WAIKIKI BEACHBOY

Waikiki Beach as it appeared in 1926. Photo courtesy of Jerry Hallinan.

*For my family, especially my parents,
my friends, and all those who believe
in Hawaii's past and try to breathe its spirit
into the present.*

Text copyright © 1989, Grady Timmons

All photographs remain the property of
their respective owners.

Published by Editions Limited
111 Royal Circle
Honolulu, Hawaii 96816

Produced by Gaylord H. Wilcox and David A. Rick

Designed by Steve Shrader

With contributions from Charles Lambert

First Printing October 1989

Second Printing December 1990

ISBN 0-915013-10-X

Printed in Hong Kong

WAIKIKI BEACHBOY
by Grady Timmons

Editions Limited

Surfers take off on a wave at Waikiki in the early 1920s. From the Hawaii State Archives.

CONTENTS

Dude Miller (at far left) with his Waikiki Beachboys in 1921. Photo courtesy of Gaylord Wilcox.

A 1936 Hawaii photo book. Courtesy of Moose McGillycuddy's.

FIRST BREAK
An Introduction

Without these remarkable people the island would be nothing. With them, it is a carnival. They are generous, courageous, and comic. They awake each morning to a fresh day that has forgiven the previous day's outrages. In the pursuit of money, they are irresponsible. In the pursuit of happiness, dedicated. They are the perpetual adolescents of the ocean, the playboys of the Pacific.

—James Michener, *Return to Paradise*

J ames Michener's "perpetual adolescents" were the Polynesian people of Tahiti, but he could just as well have been describing Waikiki's oldtime beachboys. Michener neatly summarized something I had often heard others say but which I had been slow to grasp—that the beachboys' enormous appeal emanated from their Polynesian warmth and charm.

When I first began work on this book, I knew that the beachboys were famous, colorful, celebrated, and talented, but I did not know if they could be considered historically important. It is true that the beachboys constitute a historically identifiable phenomenon. There was (and is) nothing quite like the Waikiki beachboys anywhere else in the world. But not much had been written about them, and much of what had been written was superficial. Stories about the beachboys had a tendency to pose a single question—*you mean they get paid for this?*

My own research, however, led me to the conclusion that the beachboys *were* important. Sometimes one finds a totally unexpected window into the history of a familiar locale. In this case, the beachboys are a window into oldtime Waikiki, for they were intimately connected to almost every aspect of it—the music, the water, the romance, the grand hotels and their celebrity guests.

Surfing and outrigger canoeing, two Hawaiian watersports that were in precipitous decline around the turn of the century, were revived in Waikiki in great part due to the beachboys. The music of Hawaii that so charmed the world during the first half of the twentieth century—much of it took its inspiration from the beach. Waikiki grew up around the beach, and tourism grew along with it, the beachboys functioning as its unofficial tourist bureau. Who greeted visitors with leis when they arrived? Who serenaded them with song and bid them tearful good-byes? Who was the life of the party and, in between, most everything else? As Charles ("Panama Dave") Baptiste used to say, "Hell, if it wasn't for us beachboys, nobody would come to Hawaii."

History does not tell us who the first beachboy was, and perhaps because of the maverick nature of the profession, there has never been much agreement on what exactly is a beachboy. University of Hawaii sociology student Henry Kim noted in his 1966 master's thesis, "The Waikiki Beachboy: Changing Attitudes and Behavior," that contemporary writers have portrayed the beachboy in "schizophrenic" terms: at one moment he is a romantic throwback to ancient Hawaii; at the next, a social parasite.

The dictionary defines a beachboy as someone whose livelihood is derived from surfing instruction and outrigger-canoe rides. But even this is a limited definition. There is a larger sense to the word, one that suggests a way of life. Men like Duke Kahanamoku, who was not a professional, were beachboys in the truest sense. They lived for the ocean and for a lifestyle centered on the beach.

The word beachboy shares a common history with Waikiki. It conjures up a romantic past: cruise ships and stateroom parties, a luxurious pink hotel, and a strip of sand once described as "curving in a gentle,

Duke Kahanamoku as a young man. Photo courtesy of the Bernice Pauahi Bishop Museum. (Opposite page) First Break at Waikiki as photographed by Tom Blake in 1929. In his 1935 book, *Hawaiian Surfboard,* Blake estimated the size of this surf to be thirty feet. Modern-day estimates are a more modest twelve to fifteen feet. Nonetheless, with waves at Waikiki today rarely exceeding ten feet, the photograph gives credence to boasts that the surf was bigger at Waikiki in the old days. Photo courtesy of Wally Froiseth.

flesh-covered arc towards Diamond Head." It brings back tandem surfing on giant redwood boards, baritone ukuleles, and nicknames like Splash Lyons, Laughing John, and Turkey Love. Although the beachboy tradition survives to this day in Waikiki, *real* beachboys are relics of an earlier era. Legend casts them as bronzed watermen with enormous charm, good humor, and musical genius—carefree, partying fools, and ardent womanizers. The legend is surprisingly close to the truth.

Waikiki's beachboys were a fascinating mix of men. They predominantly were Hawaiians and part-Hawaiians, ruled spiritually by the great swimmer, Duke Kahanamoku, and officially by William ("Chick") Daniels, a strapping six-footer with a personality as wide as the beach. Panama Dave, his comical sidekick, was designated clown prince.

Beachboys all seemed to have improbable names or nicknames and to be a bit, well, different. George ("Tough Bill") Keaweamahi, as an example, was so tough that he could pop the cap off a bottle of beer with his thumb. Joseph ("Scooter Boy") Kaopuiki had a "poi dog," or mongrel, that he taught how to surf. John ("Hawkshaw") Paia could take a ukulele, a chair, and a surfboard, catch a wave, set up the chair, and play the ukulele as he rode in toward the beach.

The nicknames contributed significantly to the lure and charm of the beachboys. Sarah Park, the *Honolulu Star-Bulletin*'s beachside reporter during the 1950s, once imagined what it would be like to introduce them all at a party. "Of course, you've met Dad," she saw herself saying. "And this is Turkey. And on your right we have another man from the beach, Sally. And have you met Steamboat? And this is Steamboat, Jr. And these are Steamboat's relatives: Tugboat, Sailboat, Lifeboat, and Rowboat."

The beachboys provided the world with much needed comic relief (what characters! everyone said). They took anxious, overachieving executives and taught them how to relax. They took their children and taught them how to surf. They took women who were recently divorced and taught them how to laugh and love again. In return, movie moguls took the beachboys to Hollywood, and entertainers such as Arthur Godfrey took them to New York. Ed Bennecke, whose family was a part owner of Shlitz beer, took them to the World Series. It is hard to imagine another group of men in any period of history who led a similarly ideal existence. In the eyes of the world, beachboys did not work for a living. They played for a living. They belonged to life's greatest profession.

"What's important to remember about the beachboys," former world surfing champion Fred Hemmings recalled, "is that it wasn't really a business for these men. It was a lifestyle. Working and taking tourists canoe surfing was incidental to the fact that they were men who had a life-long love affair with the ocean. And they lived off their own energy. They weren't usurping anybody else's juices."

The beachboys epitomized the Hawaiian way of life. Of course, not all of them were of Hawaiian blood. But they embodied the Hawaiian spirit. "These men were all little boys at heart," said Hemmings. "There

Panama Dave Baptiste, clown prince of the beachboys. Photo by Scoops Tsuzuki.

was a glow in their faces that manifested itself in everything they did. They appreciated the values of a beautiful environment, a clean ocean, sharing with their friends. Everybody now seems to be trying to measure their happiness in dollars and cents. These men never had that bottom-line mentality. They had a true appreciation for what I consider to be the finer things in life."

Not everyone, it should be noted, remembered the beachboys, or their lifestyle, so fondly. A prominent Honolulu archivist I spoke with recalled that when he was a young man growing up in the 1950s the beachboys were regarded as a joke—"a bunch of lazy male prostitutes who made their living off mainland divorcees."

Indeed, there is some question as to how happy and innocent the beachboys were. Legend says that they were carefree Hawaiians whose relationships with tourists were based on friendship, not money. But were they? Legend says that they were tireless womanizers, but there are those who maintain that the beachboys have always "lied like hell" about their sexual exploits. Contrary to popular belief, skeptics maintain that there were racial barriers that were not easily crossed by Hawaiians, along with a strict code of conduct in effect for beachboys.

The beachboy story is steeped in mystique and contradiction. I remember William ("Ox") Keaulani telling me about the time he persuaded a young woman to go moonlight surfing. It was a warm summer night, and as they paddled out into the darkness on his tandem board, Ox surreptitiously slipped off his bathing suit. Out near the reef, they caught a small but well-formed wave. When Ox told the woman to stand up on the board, she stood up. Suddenly, she turned and saw him, framed in the moonlight.

"Ox!" she screamed, a look of horror and excitement crossing her face.

"It fell off!" he shouted, laughing above the roar of the surf. Then, putting his arms around her waist and pulling her close, they rode the wave toward shore.

This book examines the beachboy legend. It covers a period of time between the opening of the Moana Hotel in 1901 and the advent of Hawaiian Statehood in 1959. For the most part, this book is an oral history; it is based on the recollections of the beachboys themselves and the people who knew them. But as in any oral history, the absolute accuracy of the information is only as reliable as the memories of the informants.

Beachboys have a tendency to exaggerate. If, at times, I have seen fit to accommodate this tendency, it is because I am concerned with communicating the lure and appeal of a unique group of men and because sometimes the only way to get at the truth is to stretch it.

I am reminded in this regard of an interview I had with French-Tahitian-Hawaiian beachboy Barry Napoleon. Napoleon's father had been captain of the lifeguards, and his family had a long history on the beach. Napoleon himself started working the beach in the 1950s, and over the years had earned a

Chick Daniels, head beachboy at the Royal Hawaiian Hotel. Photo courtesy of Bobby Daniels.

Legendary Waikiki waterman and beachboy Rabbit Kekai has made the beach his life. Photo by Jesse Bowman. (Opposite page) This circa 1946 portrait of Waikiki beachboys, taken at the Royal Hawaiian Hotel seawall, appeared on the cover of *Honolulu Magazine*'s 1982 Holiday Annual. Top, left to right: Blue Makua, Sr., Panama Dave Baptiste, Harry Robello. Bottom: Kalakaua Aylett, Chick Daniels, Curly Cornwell, and Ox Keaulani. Photo courtesy of Charlie Lambert.

reputation as a "wildcatter," as someone who operates without a license and undercuts legitimate concessionaires. He was not well regarded, he told me, and I am sure many would not consider him a reliable source. However, he had a wonderful flair for credible hyperbole.

"The oldtime beachboys were all fabulous watermen," he said as we sat talking one day at the west end of Waikiki. "Guys like Blue Makua could swim after fish in the water—and catch'em. And Steamboat. I've seen him stay in the water for eight hours. I remember once we was sitting up against his canoe. Some guy is bragging about riding big surf. He says, 'Eh, 'Boat, you can ride fifteen-foot surf?' Steamboat says, 'I don't know. I neva measure. But I tell you what, I can swim to Molokai.' And I believe he can."

The oldtime beachboys were multitalented, according to Napoleon. Rabbit Kekai had won paddleboard races in Peru, forty-mile canoe races between Oahu and Molokai, and so many surfing championships nobody could keep count. "Rabbit was in a category all by himself," he said. "You know the coconut-tree climb? Every year, Christmas day in front of the Moana Hotel, we used to have a coconut-tree climb. Time buzzer. Run up the coconut tree. Rabbit is the champion. No one is ever going to beat his record. You know why?"

I shook my head.

"Because the coconut tree has grown another ten feet already!"

"Rabbit is a champion surfer," he added, "champion canoeman, champion coconut-tree climber—"

"And a champion with the ladies?" I asked.

"Oh, yeah. Why do you think they call him Rabbit?"

Rabbit Kekai is among the last in a long line of legendary Hawaiian beachboys. During the writing of this book, I was able to talk with nearly all of the others who were still living. Although most had long since left the beach and gone their separate ways, they were still joined by a common memory of having been a part of an extraordinary time and place. Time, however, has not been kind to these men. The party at Waikiki is over, the golden years are gone. Still, I think their story is an important and instructive one. Certainly, it is worth preserving.—**G.T.**

This tinted postcard
shows the Royal Ha-
waiian Hotel as it looked
in 1928, a year after it
opened. With its pink
stucco walls, the castle-
like Royal Hawaiian was
a hotel that made the
world take notice. Cour-
tesy of the Bernice
Pauahi Bishop Museum.

Waikiki, the beachboys, and the sport of surfing made the cover of the December 15, 1938, issue of *Vogue* magazine. Well-known documentary and fashion photographer Toni Frisell achieved the unusual angle of the picture by shooting from atop a scaffold that she had built by the beachboys and mounted alongside two outrigger canoes. Photo courtesy of *Vogue*, copyright © 1938 (renewed 1966) by The Conde Nast Publications, Inc.

ADVANCE
RETAIL
TRADE
EDITION

See section opposite page 106

HOLIDAY TRAVEL
RESORT FASHIONS
DECEMBER 15, 1938
PRICE 35 CENTS

WAVES OF CHANGE
A Historical Overview

1

Now the beachboy is the final word. Without him, Waikiki would be a Coney Island with palm trees.

—Arthur Godfrey

B eachboy history, like the history of Waikiki, is a story of lost innocence. Once a symbol of the charm and character of a uniquely colorful era, the beachboy, like Waikiki itself, was forever changed by the tide of commercialism that swept in after the Second World War.

The beachboy emerged at the turn of the century in Waikiki as part of the revival of Hawaiian watersports. At that time, surfing and canoeing were at their nadir; indeed, both sports had been in decline since soon after the onset of Western contact in 1778.* During the nineteenth century, outrigger-canoe racing had been all but displaced by Western-style rowing regattas. And H.C. Bolton, writing in 1891 in the *Journal of American Folklore*, noted that he did not witness surfing until he visited the remote island of Niihau—a disturbing revelation since almost a third of the Hawaiian population resided in Waikiki. In 1892, anthropologist Nathaniel B. Emerson wrote disparagingly, "The sport of surf riding possessed a grand fascination, and for a time, it seemed as if it had a vitality all its own as a national pastime...today it is hard to find a surfboard outside our museums and private collections."

That sports of such beauty and grace fell so far so fast was as dismaying as their revival was unlikely. In 1907, Alexander Hume Ford, an eccentric promoter and former newsman from Chicago, stepped off a boat in Honolulu and began a crusade to revive the "royal sport of surfing." Ford observed that Waikiki Beach was becoming closed to the "small boy of limited means." Private residences and a posh new hotel were choking off access to what already was a small strip of sand between two seawalls.

Ford decided to do something about it. He first enlisted the support of Jack London, a famous writer whom he had introduced to surfing and who at the time was sojourning in Waikiki. Next, he negotiated a twenty-year lease on a small plot of land adjoining the Moana Hotel, relocated two grass shacks, and founded the Outrigger Canoe Club. Membership fees for boys were set at five dollars a year. "Such dues," wrote Ford, "made it possible for every kid with guts to live at least half the day fighting the surf."

Ford then tried to enlist as the club's first captain the noted Honolulu waterman George ("Dad") Center, who later became the coach of the 1920 United States Olympic swim team. "He scorned the surf," Ford wrote. "It took me two years to persuade Dad to come to Waikiki to take a look-see."

When Dad finally came, he stayed. Indeed, he was part of a growing twentieth-century phenomenon: the discovery of surfing by *haoles* ("Caucasians"). Ford, who had by then started *Mid-Pacific Magazine*, was there to chronicle surfing's growing popularity.

When it had been fairly demonstrated that the white man could learn all the secrets of the Hawaiian-born, the beach at Waikiki took on a new aspect. The people of Honolulu turned

The beachboy and the Hawaiian maiden were once popular images used to sell Waikiki. This promotional piece by Hawaii artist John Kelly first appeared on the back cover of a 1929 Hawaii Tourists Bureau publication. From the DeSoto Brown Collection. (Opposite page) Duke Kahanamoku (standing at left) and other prominent Waikiki watermen near the Seaside Hotel in 1914. Photo by Ray Jerome Baker, from the Baker-Van Dyke Collection.

* The decline in ancient Hawaiian watersports has been attributed to the near annihilation of the Hawaiian population by foreign disease and to the arrival of Christian missionaries in 1820, who viewed surfing and canoe racing as idle pursuits that promoted nudity and gambling.

their attention to the reviving of the old-time water sports. Hundreds learned to ride the surfboard.... During visits of the fleets, surfing carnivals were held [and] small boys and men, to the astonishment of the jackies, came in upon their boards, on their heads. At night time the expert surfers carried red light contrivances on the bows of their boards, and in the caps on their heads, matches, with which they set off the glaring colored lights just before they caught some monster wave, and then those on the beach were treated to the sight of radiant gods of the sea outlined against the darkness, standing upon the white crests of the waves, which they rode... erect and elated.

Ford's attempt to revive ancient Hawaiian watersports was successful, but his new club had a curious flaw: it was almost exclusively Caucasian in membership. A rival club was formed in 1911, one composed almost exclusively of Hawaiians or part-Hawaiians. Called Hui Nalu, or "Club of the Waves," it had as one of its founders the twenty-one-year-old Duke Kahanamoku, who was beginning to make a name for himself as a surfer and swimmer. Unlike Outrigger, Hui Nalu had no clubhouse. Members met beneath a hau tree on the lawn of the Moana Hotel, and dues were only one dollar a year. The Moana Bathhouse, located in the hotel basement, served as their locker room.

The two clubs were friendly rivals, with some members belonging to both. A certain ethnic pride, however, lay at the heart of their competition: haoles vied with Hawaiians in ancient water sports which were considered to be the domain of the latter. Contests between the two clubs eventually contributed to a modern-day renaissance of the sport of canoe racing.

The two clubs are also integral to the beachboy story. Tourists coming to Waikiki in the early 1900s were entranced by the sport of surfing. To slide through the water in a canoe or to stand on a board and be hurled toward shore was to experience the rarest of thrills. The men of Hui Nalu and Outrigger had the skills and equipment to teach them how to perform these feats.

Many of the early Hui Nalu members became known as the first beachboys, and most of the more-recent beachboys came from their ranks. Outrigger members, although some of the best watermen on the beach, generally did not take to the profession. Their club, which became a prominent social organization, developed in a different way. Realizing that money could be made from the increasing traffic of tourists, it later took advantage of its strategic location between the beach's two major hotels and started Waikiki's second, and eventually major, beach service. The move helped the club to survive financially. It also benefitted the beachboys, providing them with equipment and a place of employment.

But the institutionalizing of the beachboy probably had less to do with Hui Nalu and Outrigger than with the advent of tourism. The first beachboy is thought to have appeared on Waikiki Beach soon after

Edward, the Prince of Wales, created quite a stir when he stayed at the Moana Hotel and went for an outrigger canoe ride during a 1920 visit. Photo by Ray Jerome Baker, from the Baker-Van Dyke Collection.

the first major resort, the Moana Hotel, was completed in 1901. At that time, most of what is now Waikiki comprised acres of bush and swampland (its major thoroughfare, Kalakaua Avenue, was a crushed coral road), and it was far removed from downtown Honolulu.

The Moana helped open up Waikiki. The posh new hostelry, built in a beaux-arts style of architecture, was distinguished by a giant banyan tree in the courtyard fronting the beach and by a marvelous wooden pier that extended some three hundred feet out into the water. In advertisements that appeared as early as 1906, the Moana was proclaiming surfing and canoeing to be exciting vehicles of sport for tourists. But it was almost another decade before an enterprising part-Hawaiian named Edward Kenneth Kaleleihealani ("Dude") Miller made an arrangement with the hotel and launched the beach's first concession.

With the exception of Duke Kahanamoku, Dude (pronounced Dudie) was the premier beachboy of his era. He was a champion board rider and the first captain of Hui Nalu. He was among the first to take tourists out in an outrigger canoe, and at a time when divers used glass boxes for masks and wielded long hand-held spears, he was the best spearfisherman on the beach.

Dude was also a gifted musician. He played piano and an assortment of stringed instruments, and his orchestra, the Dude Miller Band, performed in the evenings at the Moana Hotel.

Dude was the prototypical beachboy, and on the beach and on the dance floor he set standards for dress and conduct that lasted for decades. "You know how Dude and his gang dressed?" recalled Joe Akana, born in 1907 and the beachboys' elder statesman. "Pongee suits from China, the material. Off-white. Flat, ivory buttons. They had tufts, but they kept a beautiful crease. They had white ties and shirts and white Panama hats. Shee! What they looked like in those days."

The men of Hui Nalu respectfully referred to Dude as "The Commodore." He was a fearsome leader whom they loved even as he dominated them. Dude made his beachboys wear uniforms. He made sure they were clean-cut and clean-shaven, and when he was on duty there was no drinking, no gambling, and no letting your hands stray over female tourists. "That guy controlled beachboys more than any guy I know," recalled Alan ("Turkey") Love. "He didn't just restrict gambling on the beach. He restricted just plain cards. Checkers. You couldn't. When I was a kid, I used to have to go sit out on the road if the guys were shooting craps. I was the lookout. And when I saw his car, I ran down the beach."

Dude Miller's beachboys were known as the Moana Bathhouse Gang, and in addition to manning the canoes and providing surfing instruction, a big part of their job was keeping the beach a safe, clean place for tourists. This was not always easy. Youth gangs in Waikiki and throughout Honolulu during the 1920s were very territorial, and skirmishes among them or with visiting sailors were common. Although the

The Moana Pier at sunrise, 1922. The small pavillion at the end of the pier is where the beachboys gathered to sing and play music on Sunday evenings. Photo by Tai Sing Loo, from the Baker-Van Dyke Collection.

KEONI EHUKAI ~NUTE~ FRED HILO DAVID

Different generations of beachboys (photos counter clockwise from bottom left): The Hui Nalu surf club, circa 1920 (back row from left): Dude Miller, W. Noinoa, Knute Cotrell, Fred Wilhelm, Hilo Boyd, Harold Castle, David Kahanamoku, Steamboat Bill Keaweamahi, Hiram Anahu. Second row: M. Dowd, Kim Wai, John D. Kaupiko, J. Hjorth, Joe Bishaw, William Kahanamoku, Zen Genoves, Aude Holstein, Lew Henderson, Sam Kahanamoku, unknown. Front row: Pua Kealoha, Ludy Langer, E. Gliebtrey, Stubby Kruger, Duke Kahanamoku, H. Prieste, H. Beckley, H. Awano. Photo courtesy of Harry Robello. The Waikiki Beach Patrol in 1935 (from left): Chick Daniels, Boss Makua, a French movie star, Joe Minor, Sally Hale, and Bill Mullahey. Photo courtesy of Charlie Lambert. The Outrigger Beach Services in 1952 (from left): Sally Hale, Turkey Love, Johnny Hollinger, Steamboat Mokuahi, Jr., a young boy, Steamboat Mokuahi, Sr., unknown, Tarzan Smith and (kneeling) Panama Dave Baptiste and Philip Kaaihue. Photo courtesy of Steamboat Mokuahi, Sr. Prominent Waikiki beachboys, circa 1945 (from left): Turkey Love, Blue Makua, Sr., Laughing John, unknown, Panama Dave Baptiste, Curly Cornwell, and Chick Daniels. Photo courtesy of Charlie Lambert.

The historic Waikiki Tavern, a popular beachboy hangout that was located on the Diamond Head side of the Moana Hotel, as it appeared in 1950. Photo by Ray Jerome Baker, from the Baker-Van Dyke Collection. (Opposite page) The antics of beachboy comedian Pua Kealoha (standing) and friends, bring to mind the words of Frances Parkinson Keyes, who wrote in 1926 that beachboys often "array themselves in outlandish costumes and parade along the beach, indulging in all sorts of pranks and buffoonery, their own childlike enjoyment in these pastimes as great as the amusement they afford to others." Circa 1933 photo from the Sawtelle-Van Dyke Collection.

scraps usually ended up as quickly forgotten incidents, many still remember the day when the famed cruise ship, *Great Northern*, and its all-German crew, pulled into Honolulu Harbor.

"They came marching down Kalakaua Avenue, about eighteen or twenty of them," recalled Louis Kahanamoku, one of Duke's five brothers. "The head guy gave a whistle. He yells, 'Charge!' But we were ready. And we were fast. Bam. Bam. Bam. The whole thing happened so fast. Pretty soon the head guy gave another whistle. 'Retreat!'"

By most accounts, the beachboys won that encounter by a knockout. But the truth is that they were not much given to violence. Fight? The beachboys would rather drink and laugh and make music. Frances Parkinson Keyes, writing in *Good Housekeeping* in 1926, noted that "in their leisure moments, the beachboys, who act as lifeguards, array themselves in outlandish costumes and parade along the beach, indulging in all sorts of pranks and buffoonery, their own childlike enjoyment in these pastimes quite as great as the amusement they afford to others. In the evenings, they gather at the end of the Moana pier to sing, without money and without price, before an audience that completely fills the Moana Hotel pleasure pier, and the long approach to it."

Music was as integral to the beachboys' life as the water. In the late afternoons they serenaded along the waterfront with their guitars and ukuleles. In the evenings, they performed in the hotels or retired to the Waikiki Tavern, where they could enjoy one another's company and engage in revelry and song. Kenneth Brown, a prominent part-Hawaiian whose father and uncle were both early members of Hui Nalu, recalled that the beachboys seemed to communicate through music.* "Music was almost a preferred method of communicating," he said. "When they sang together, they were together, spiritually. And the songs. Some happy songs, some dirty songs, some serious songs, some sad songs. Song meant a lot to them. When they weren't out surfing, they'd be sitting around singing."

The beachboys who ruled Waikiki before 1930 probably came closest to the romantic ideal. They led a conspicuously languorous existence. The job of beachboy was not really a job at all but something they did during their off hours for little or no money. Tourism had only two seasons, winter and summer. "In between there was nothing," recalled Turkey Love. "And I mean nothing."

After the opening of the Royal Hawaiian Hotel in 1927, things began to change. The castlelike hostelry, built by the Matson Steamship and Navigation Company, stood front and center on Waikiki Beach, with pink stucco walls and more than eight hundred palm trees. The Royal Hawaiian was a hotel that made the world take notice. Along with Matson's new seven-deck luxury cruiser, the *Malolo*, it was part of a travel package that succeeded in attracting the rich and famous: millionaires Nelson Rockefeller and Henry Ford II, and a host of Hollywood stars that included Douglas Fairbanks and Mary Pickford.

Waikiki was suddenly the rage, an exotic playground where the rich could get away from the pressures and pretensions of their normal lives. They often came for months at a stretch. Many brought their own

* Kenneth Brown, a well-known Honolulu architect and businessman, is the great grandson of John Ii, a gifted statesman and one of the leading Hawaiian figures of the nineteenth century. His uncle, Francis Ii Brown, was an internationally renowned golfer during the 1920s and 1930s.

cars, and some, such as tobacco heiress Doris Duke, built fabulous mansions. The visitor count, which stood at sixteen thousand in 1930, doubled in the decade leading up to the Second World War. Life was good (despite the Depression), and Waikiki was at a crucial stage of development. The bullrushes and duckponds were gone, drained off as part of a major reclamation project during the 1920s. In their place was a quiet, residential neighborhood where flowers bloomed and palms swayed against the sky. People parked their cars on Kalakaua Avenue and simply walked in. Few buildings were more than three stories tall.

For all its charm, however, Waikiki was not the haven of racial serenity it has sometimes been made out to be. Indeed, in 1931 Thalia Massie, the socialite wife of a Navy lieutenant, reported being raped at a beach near Waikiki. Five youths of various ethnic backgrounds were charged with the crime but later acquitted. Soon after, Massie's outraged husband, mother, and two Navy men kidnapped and killed Joe Kahahawai, one of the accused men.

The Massie Case, as it came to be called, generated national headlines (in the end, famed defense attorney Clarence Darrow achieved a kind of tawdry victory when the territorial governor commuted a ten-year sentence for Kahahawai's killers to an hour in jail), and its racial overtones were strongly felt on the beach. In an article published by the *International News Service,* Dorothy Mackaill, a noted Hollywood film actress who frequented the islands, blamed the incident on the activities between American white women and Hawaiian beachboys at Waikiki. "It had to come," she wrote.

> The beachboys…have had many romances with rich American women, who have gone to the islands as tourists and been enthralled with its Eden-like fascination. These affairs have been invited by the white women visitors….[who] lie on the beach….in abbreviated bathing suits and permit the "beach boys" to rub them with coconut oil so they will receive a good tan….The killing of Joe Kahahawai is deplorable. It is a tribute to the real Hawaiian people that none of the men accused of attacking Mrs. Massie was a *Kanaka* [Hawaiian]. The five men were mixed breed….[But] what can we expect of these people when they see Kanakas openly receiving the attentions of American white women?

A direct result of the Massie case was the formation of the Waikiki Beach Patrol under the auspices of the Outrigger Canoe Club. In 1934, the financially troubled club approached noted Island waterman Bill Mullahey about establishing a service similar to the Jones Beach Lifeguard Patrol he had operated in New York.* Outrigger wanted to consolidate the beachfront—buy up equipment and bring together individual entrepreneurs into a single, responsible concession.

Many, but not all, of the beachboys joined the new Beach Patrol, which along with Hui Nalu helped to impose order on the beach. At first Mullahey, and later Louis ("Sally") Hale, ran the concession, with

* Bill Mullahey, who became Pacific regional director for Pan American World Airways, is described by Eugene Burdick in his 1961 book, *The Blue of Capricorn,* as a man who had been born in the Pacific and who possessed "one of the keenest minds and sweeping imaginations to be found anywhere."

Bing Crosby dances with a hula maiden in a scene from the 1936 movie, *Waikiki Wedding.* Photo courtesy of Joe Akana. (Opposite page) During a visit to Hawaii in 1935, Shirley Temple was named honorary captain of the Waikiki Beach Patrol. Photo courtesy of Joanne Makalena Takatsugi.

The Moana Hotel became a rest and recreation center for the military during World War II. Photo by Herbert Bauer, courtesy of the Bernice Pauahi Bishop Museum.

Waikiki visitor Shirley Temple serving as its honorary captain. The men of the Beach Patrol were both colorful and honorable. As a general rule, they did not hustle tourists. They worked their own hours and the money they made from tips, lessons, and canoe rides (there were no paid salaries) was sometimes considerable. The one-hundred dollar handshake, for instance, signaled a job well done, and boat day, when guests departed, was "mail" day: every beachboy received an envelope stuffed with cash.

Michael Mullahey, son of Beach Patrol founder Bill Mullahey, recalled that the special appeal of the beachboy was that he did not have a hidden agenda. He was a kind of all-purpose ambassador and a visitor's invaluable link to Waikiki. "Waikiki at that time was a very, very healing place," he said. "You would come there because you instinctively knew that's where you needed to be if you wanted to rest, if you needed to get well. The waters were beneficent, the breezes were soothing, the whole vibration of the place was something that just drew you in.

"The people who came there really experienced relaxation, and in the beachboys they found a group of men who were funny, sharing, open, kind. You'd walk into this place, see these marvelous waves breaking out on the reef, and say to yourself, 'Gee, I'd really like to go out there.' And this big brown fella would walk up who's got a smile on his face—I mean, he's not going to eat you for dinner—and he'd say, 'Yeah, I can turn you on to that.' And away you'd go. You're in.

"The beachboys were the ones who taught me, and a lot of other people, to *see* the place. Because they really saw it. It was their place, and they were willing to share it."

The Second World War hit hard at Waikiki. Within hours of the Japanese attack on Pearl Harbor, Hawaii was under martial law. Huge coils of barbed wire soon encircled the island of Oahu. A blackout went into effect after sunset, and any street lights left burning were shot out by the Army. (Rabbit Kekai recalled that eventually gun emplacements were installed every couple of hundred yards on Diamond Head and that gunners fired warning shots over the heads of surfers caught in the water after curfew.) All of Matson's passenger liners and cargo ships were pressed into the service of the U.S. wartime fleet, while the swank confines of the Royal Hawaiian became a rest-and-recreation center for the Navy. Tourism came to an abrupt halt.

Beachboys took other jobs or joined the war effort. Chick Daniels went to work at an underground fuel storage tank beneath Oahu's Red Hill. Panama Dave drove a jeep for the Army. Turkey Love labored at the Pearl Harbor dry docks. After the war was over, many of the beachboys never returned. The war changed Hawaii, and Waikiki in particular. In its aftermath, the Islands were swept into the modern world, their innocence lost. Gone were the days when only the moneyed and leisured class traveled to the Islands by ocean liner. Air travel was ushering in a new era.

Nevertheless, in 1946 the Royal Hawaiian was refurbished at a cost of $2 million and, for a while, the party that had begun there so many years before resumed. In the postwar years, the Outrigger Beach Services became Waikiki's lone concession while the job of beachboy became a full-time endeavor, more a business than a lifestyle. The 1950s saw a new influx of the rich and famous, including department-store millionaires David May and Alfred Bloomingdale. Frank Sinatra and Ava Gardner came for their honeymoon. John Wayne came to make movies. Red Skelton arrived with his son who was dying of leukemia; among his son's last requests was one asking to be taught surfboard riding by a Waikiki beachboy.

Arthur Godfrey, who had first fallen in love with Hawaii as a CBS correspondent during the war, began to extol its virtues on his national television and radio broadcasts. In 1950, he brought Duke Kahanamoku, Chick Daniels, and Splash Lyons with him to New York to entertain the nation. Scheduled for a two-week stint on Godfrey's show, the trio was held over and stayed a month.

The beachboys were becoming famous, and so were some of Waikiki's other characters. One was a stray "poi dog," or mongrel, named Sandy, who was adopted by Joseph ("Scooter Boy") Kaopuiki and taught to surf. Sandy rode the breakers every day. He was billed as the "dog-gonest" surfer you have ever seen—and he was not always easy to please. If you were to take him out and catch a bad wave, he would growl. If you proved to be a poor surfer, he would jump off your board and swim in.

A news photo of Sandy surfing with Scooter Boy appeared in newspapers across the country, and *You Asked For It!* filmed him for television. John ("Menehune") Ohelo, a long-time beach attendant at the Royal Hawaiian, recalled that Sandy became a world-famous beachdog. He could go anywhere in Waikiki, scratch on any door and get a place to sleep, go into any restaurant and be served. "Hell," Menehune said, "the beachboys used to follow him to dinner."

Sandy became a symbol of Waikiki's carefree lifestyle. When he died in the late 1950s of natural causes, a large flotilla of canoes took his ashes out to sea. Menehune, who attended the ceremony, recalled standing next to a tourist couple from New York.

"What's going on?" the husband asked him.

"A funeral," said Menehune.

"Oh. Must be a very important person."

"No, just a dog."

The man turned to his wife. "That does it," he said. "We're moving to Hawaii."

More and more people were coming—and moving—to the Islands, but they had less money to spend. By 1955, the tourist count was approaching one hundred thousand, and new hotels were being constructed everywhere. At the Ewa end of Waikiki (the end farthest from Diamond Head), Henry J. Kaiser built the Hilton Hawaiian Village, carving out a new beach with its own lagoon. At the Diamond Head end, an area known as Kuhio Beach was greatly expanded to create more beach frontage for the increasing number of visitors.

Another concession, Earl Akana's Hale Auau Surfboards, was opened on Kuhio Beach to service the new visitors. Akana's arrival marked a major change in Waikiki. His beachboys were a new breed, and

their skills as watermen, not to mention their treatment of tourists, often left something to be desired. Relegated to a second-class status because their end of the beach was not frequented by the more-affluent tourists, they resorted to hustling.

For a buck-fifty they rented out old, hollow boards, pulling the cork from the boards as they launched tourists into the surf. After two or three waves the boards filled with water, and the tourists were forced to return to the beach.

"Hey, there's something wrong with my board!" they would complain.

"No wonder, you lost the cork! You owe us a quarter," Akana's men would reply.

Veteran beachboys at the Outrigger Beach Service resented these mavericks. The oldtimers were proud of their profession and took a dim view of openly soliciting tourists. It just was not done. But the worst was yet to come.

Competition on the beach grew increasingly fierce. It was not long before Hale Auau attained a certain respectability in comparison with an even newer group of beachboys known as "wildcatters"—freelancers who went into business after setting up an umbrella and a few surfboards. Their ranks included vagrants and criminals.

Wildcatters were a constant source of friction. They exploited the beach to their financial advantage, undercutting legitimate concessionaires and stealing business. Fights soon broke out on the beach over territory. An imaginary line separated Kuhio Beach from the beach between the Moana and the Royal, but wildcatters ventured across it. "The Outrigger guys had no problem making a living," one wildcatter recalled. "For them, it was all romance. Rebels like us didn't get to sit around and cocktail with the tourists. We never laid out in the sun and made all those big tips. The only big money we made came when we attacked that side."

The word beachboy began to take on a new connotation: "beach bum." In 1959, Arthur Godfrey felt compelled to render a scathing appraisal. "Waikiki's become a Coney Island with palm trees," he told the press. "All you get on the beach are insults and insubordination....It makes a guy who loves this place like I do want to cry."

Godfrey's outburst resulted in a crackdown. Beachboys began to be licensed and were required to demonstrate levels of competence. Still, the wildcatters remained, and the modern-day beachboy was born, more a product of the times than anything else.

Statehood arrived in 1959, and with it the ease and popularity of jet travel. The visitor count that year was a quarter of a million. Within the next decade, the people and places that gave Waikiki its sense of history began to disappear. Matson sold its four hotels and got out of the tourist business. The Waikiki Tavern was torn down, and the Outrigger Canoe Club relocated more than a mile down the beach toward Diamond Head. Chick retired from the Royal. Panama, Duke, and others passed away. One by one, their ashes were taken out to sea, scattered just beyond a point the beachboys call First Break. Turning back the clock it is here, out where the big surf crests and the turquoise water becomes a deep blue, that our story really begins.

Duke Kahanamoku, Johnny Weismuller, and Buster Crabbe were all on hand when the Waikiki Natatorium, a saltwater swimming pool located near the flank of Diamond Head, opened on August 24, 1927. The date was the Duke's 37th birthday. Today, the abandonned pool is a remnant of a bygone Waikiki. Photo by Franco Salmoiraghi. (Following spread) Even in his sixties, beachboy Rabbit Kekai, pictured here on a wave at Waikiki, remains among the elite of Hawaii's surfers. Photo © Don King, Pacific Ocean Stock.

Few Waikiki beachboys could perform better on the old-style surfboards than Scooter Boy Kaopuiki, pictured here in 1954 with his famous surfing poi dog, Sandy. Photo by Clarence "Mac" Maki; hand-colored by Ron Hudson.

WATERMEN
The Call of the Surf

2

Far out to the opalescent horizon stretches the ocean in broad bands of jeweled color—turquoise, sapphire, emerald, amethyst; and curving around it like a tawny topaz girdle presses the hard, firm sand of the shore. The pearly surf, diamond crested, sweeps in with a swift, strong surging unlike any sound I have ever heard before; and balanced in superb symmetry on their surfboards, the beach boys come riding in toward land.

—Frances Parkinson Keyes

Waikiki Beach is a marvel of nature, that rare place where circumstances have wrought a nearly perfect aquatic arena. Hidden beneath the surface is a gradually tapered shelf—a flat, smooth ocean bottom running out toward Diamond Head at an angle. On a perfect day years ago, the different surfs which formed out on the reef lined up along this shelf, sliding in toward the beach. From Diamond Head it was a left slide: Castle's Surf, a towering body of water more than a mile off shore, was followed by Public's, Cunha's, Queen's, and finally Canoe's. Each surf merged with the next, breaking evenly along the angle of the shelf, so that the skilled surfer could move diagonally across them, not unlike a man stepping from stone to stone across a stream.

Toward the Ewa side of the beach (the side opposite Diamond Head) First Break, Popular's Surf, Blow Hole, and Kanakopia's Surf slid right toward shore.

The degree of skill required to ride these different breaks increased as one moved seaward. Thus, there was something for everyone. The baby surf at Canoe's—so named because it was here that the outriggers shuttled back and forth—was a benign, easy roller, perfect for beginners. Cunha's was decidedly more challenging, one of Waikiki's more popular board-surfing spots when it was breaking. Castle's Surf, where waves were said to have reached heights of twenty feet, was strictly for experts. Very few got that far.

Duke Kahanamoku once described the classic Waikiki wave as being "long in forming, slow to break, and running for great distances." The prevailing wind, a light off-shore breeze, blew into the face of the wave, pushing and holding it up. For these reasons Waikiki was ideal for canoe surfing. If Waikiki's ocean bottom had fallen abruptly off into deeper water, creating a wave that rose up suddenly and fell just as fast, outrigger canoes would have been out of business. On a steep wave a canoe pitches forward out of control, the water hammering it to the ocean floor like a large wooden peg.

No other beach anywhere was as well suited for both board riding and canoe surfing. No other beach was equally suitable for diving, fishing, sailing, sunbathing, and swimming. Waikiki's weather was sunny and dry, its water shallow and warm, free from undertow and sharks. Gentle ocean swells and channels in the reef made it easy for surfers and sailboats to get in and out. The one feature that did not contribute to good swimming—the coral reef—made the area a wonderful fishing grounds (it was once a royal fishing grounds). As a marine environment, Waikiki was almost ideal. The conjunction of sand and flat reef enabled squid, lobster, *moi*, *papio*, and an assortment of reef fish to flourish.

Unfortunately, Waikiki is not all it once was. While there is now a bigger, wider beach that holds more people, the addition of groins and sand have had adverse effects. Much of the sand has drifted out onto the reef and sectioned off the surf. As a result, the classic Waikiki ride—from outside to shore break—is no longer possible. The area has suffered from excessive fishing. Waikiki has been largely fished out since about the 1960s. Moreover, the added sand has filled in squid and lobster holes and, along with sewage

The Matson Navigation Company, which once owned the Moana and Royal Hawaiian hotels, used the image of the surfer in many of its promotional pieces. From the Baker-Van Dyke Collection. (Opposite page) Legendary Waikiki beachboy Steamboat Mokuahi had what is commonly referred to as "squid eye," the ability while diving to look at a coral reef and know which holes contain squid. Photo by Wally Young, courtesy of Steamboat Mokuahi.

outfall, has damaged much of the reef.

Oldtime beachboys still talk about how Waikiki used to be: how you could catch a wave and ride it nearly all the way to the beach; how there were days when you could not see the ocean bottom because the water was thick with fish. Back then, back before Waikiki became overladen with concrete and crime became a problem, a boy could store his surfboard between the roots of the giant banyan tree at Kuhio Beach and know that it would be safe. He could feast on fish or on the fruit that grew wild all around him: coconuts, bananas, mangoes, and dates. Such feasting was called a "tropical lunch."

In those days, there came a time in the life of every boy who loved the beach when Waikiki called to him. The beach became his second home, his daytime haunt, his field of blue. Baldwin ("Blue") Makua, Sr., was six when he began surfing at Waikiki on his mother's wooden ironing board. Rabbit Kekai was about the same age when he first cut the top off an apple crate and used it to go *paipo* boarding. Ox Keaulani was eleven when he said good-bye to his mother, explaining that he wished to become a beachboy. At night he slept on the sand or, if it rained, underneath a canoe. At age eleven, the beach was his life.

When Wally Froiseth was a boy, he felt the same way. Froiseth was one of the "Tavern Boys" who used to hang out on the Kuhio side of the beach. A member of neither Hui Nalu nor the Outrigger Canoe Club, he helped to start a rival organization, the Waikiki Surf Club. He was among the first to venture outside Waikiki and attempt the big winter surf on Oahu's North and West shores; he was also among the first to cross the treacherous Molokai Channel in a canoe. In 1959 he won the Makaha Surfing Championships, an event he helped to organize. Froiseth only briefly made his living off the beach, but he was a beachboy just the same. His first love was the ocean.

"People who really loved the beach—a day couldn't go by without your going down there," he recalled. "Even if it was just for five or ten minutes, to look at the surf, you had to go and satisfy that craving. I remember one day it got so bad. I was living up in Manoa Valley....It had been a couple of days since I'd been to the beach, and when I got home I just flew out the door and started running toward Waikiki. It was hot and I was in no condition—I mean, I could swim a mile but I wasn't a runner—that when I got there I collapsed from heat prostration. But I just had to get down to the water. I couldn't sleep at night unless I'd been to the beach. And I wasn't the only one who felt that way."

What is it that draws a man to water? Is it the lure of high-risk adventure? A need for refuge? The appeal of an uncharted frontier? Freedom? Is salt air charged with the scent of challenge? Is getting wet a never-ending rite of purification?

A love for the ocean was the common bond among beachboys. Not all beachboys were gifted musicians or great lovers, but nearly all were agile watermen. No doubt being or feeling Hawaiian had something to

Between 1958 and 1963, beachboy Blue Makua, Sr., shown here on the July 1958 cover of *Paradise of the Pacific* magazine, steered the Waikiki Surf Club to six consecutive victories in the grueling forty-mile Molokai-to-Oahu canoe race. From the Baker-Van Dyke Collection, printed with permission from *Honolulu Magazine.*

do with this predilection. In the same way that some cultures valued runners and others hunters, the ancient Hawaiians valued oceanmen, whom they believed had come from the sea. The ocean was one of the gods. It was a source of protein, a field for sport, a sanctuary. It was a friend, not an adversary, and perhaps for this reason the ancient Hawaiians were in tune with its mysteries. Living on islands, the Hawaiians were surrounded, defined, sustained, and renewed by the ocean.

According to Tommy Holmes, a noted Pacific maritime ethnohistorian and author of *The Hawaiian Canoe*, the ocean held a special place in a Hawaiian's heart. "He loved that ocean—in all its moods, in all its offerings," said Holmes in an interview. "The ancients derived their sense of well-being and peace, their sense of joy, from the ocean. When the culture was eroding, they could still retain their bonds to the old ways via the ocean. The spiritual aspect was very real. On a daily basis, they renewed their spirit with the ocean."

The ancient Polynesians crossed seven thousand miles of trackless ocean without the benefit of modern navigational instruments. Their instruments were their bodies. Their canoes were, Holmes wrote in *The Hawaiian Canoe*, "the most versatile and seaworthy roughwater craft ever designed or built by any culture."

The modern-day catamaran, designed and built in 1948 by Waikiki waterman Woody Brown, was fashioned after the giant double-hulled canoes of the ancient Polynesians. Brown had consulted old accounts and sketches and concluded that the Polynesians were remarkably ingenious. "A thousand years before Captain Cook, the Polynesians were sailing canoes against the wind with an asymmetrical hull," he pointed out. "They had designed an airplane wing in the water. They even had streamlined masts."

The ancient Hawaiians' knowledge and mastery of the ocean stagger the imagination, and documented accounts of their exploits abound. In his book, *The Works of the People of Old*, noted nineteenth-century Hawaiian historian Samuel Kamakau wrote, "I have seen a man skilled in steering sharks ride a shark like a horse, turning it this way and that as it carried him to land—where he killed it."

In another astonishing passage he described a method used to catch eels which has the fisherman lying face down among rocks, his arm extended. The fisherman's fingers are held wide apart, his thumb pressing crabmeat into the palm of his hand. "The head of the eel would appear between the fingers as it came to eat from the palm. The fisherman would clamp his fingers together, and the head of the eel would be

Kaniau Evans, one of the original members of the Hui Nalu surf club, photographed and hand-colored this shot of a group of beachboys beside their canoe. Circa 1920, from the collection of Kaniau Evans.

caught fast. If all the spaces between the fingers were filled, then six eels might be caught at one time. As their tails thrashed about, the fisherman would bite the eels in the middle of the back, and their wide open mouths would bite him on the cheek, or the neck, or on the ear lobes. The eel snarer went on with this odd way of fishing until his bag was full."

John Turnbull, author of *A Voyage Round the World in the Years 1800-1804*, was astounded by practices he observed among native Hawaiian divers. Hired to nail copper sheets to a ship's bottom, the divers would remain submerged for up to four minutes at a stretch, a feat Turnbull scarcely would have believed had he not seen it himself.

Their boldness and dexterity in diving is perhaps unrivaled in any part of the world....I have heard from Mr. Young, that Tamahama [Kamehameha I], in the early part of his career, being one day on board, requested of the captain an anvil, an article of which he stood in great need....[He] was told that he should have one on the condition that his divers should simply bear it up in ten fathoms water. To this he instantly agreed and the anvil was thrown into the sea. Tamahama immediately sent some of his people down after it....but they found it somewhat too heavy. Unwilling however to abandon so great a treasure, they continued their efforts, and, after long and repeated exertions, succeeded in rolling the anvil along the bottom of the sea, for about half a mile, relieving each other alternately till they gained the beach, and were received by their countrymen with the loudest applause. These and similar exertions....are often attended with dangerous consequences to their health. On their reappearing on the surface of the water, we observed their faces to be greatly swelled, their eyes red and inflamed, and blood discharging profusely from their nose and ears. In a short time, however, they recover their usual state, and are ready to repeat the same exertion, and incur the same or greater injury.

Turnbull made an additional observation about the Hawaiians: "Their fondness for the water is indeed singular...as if it was their native element."

"The ancient Hawaiians were probably the greatest watermen the world has ever known," Tommy Holmes maintained. "And the beachboys, by extension, were the last carryover. They were pre-eminent watermen. And not only as canoeists and surfers. They were world-class swimmers. Superb fishermen. As divers, they were incredible."

The early beachboys in particular were not far removed from the ways of their ancestors. A century of missionary influence could not dull their aquatic skills or love for the sea. During the first half of the twentieth century, Hawaiian water sports enjoyed a resurgence; at the center of this resurgence was the Waikiki beachboy. Waikiki became center stage for a Hawaiian renaissance. Indeed, it became the center of the aquatic world.

The coach and eleven members of the 1920 U.S. Olympic swim team were from Hawaii. Shown here (clockwise from back row) are: Warren Kealoha, Ludy Langer, Duke Kahanamoku, coach Dad Center, Pua Kealoha, Helen Moses Cassidy, and "Wild Wild Bill" Harris. From the Hawaii State Archives.

Tom Blake, a Waikiki waterman originally from Wisconsin, revolutionized surfboard design in 1926 when he accidentally invented the "hollow" surfboard. Blake made all six of the boards shown here. The four at left are examples of the "hollow" board; the two at right are paddleboards. Photo courtesy of the Bernice Pauahi Bishop Museum.

Circa 1906: Waikiki beachboy Dude Miller is among the first to take tourists for an outrigger-canoe ride, a sport that is catching on in popularity. Canoe surfing is being preserved and revived at Waikiki, and the beachboy is almost solely responsible.

1907: A Hawaiian-Irish beachboy named George Freeth is invited to California to demonstrate the art of surfing. Billed as "the man who can walk on water," Freeth is the well-known Waikiki waterman about whom Jack London wrote, "He is Mercury—a brown Mercury. His heels are winged, and in them is the swiftness of the sea." It was Freeth, along with Alexander Hume Ford, who had taught London to surf. As a result of the California surfing exhibition, Freeth comes to be known as "the first surfer in the United States."

1911: Duke Kahanamoku shatters the existing world 100-yard freestyle swimming record with a clocking of 55.4 seconds in Honolulu Harbor—a record that goes unrecognized by the Amateur Athletic Union. A year later Duke wins his first Olympic gold medal at Stockholm, Sweden. Waikiki, heretofore the home of the surfer, is now the home of the world's fastest swimmer. Playing down his achievements to the European press, Duke maintains that he is "just a beachboy from Waikiki."

1920: The Duke wins two more gold medals at the Olympic Games in Antwerp, Belgium. He leads a Hawaiian sweep of the first four places in the 100-meter freestyle, and is joined on the victory stand after winning the 800-meter relay by Pua Kealoha, a beachboy teammate. In all, eleven members of the U.S. Olympic swim team are from Hawaii. The coach is Outrigger's Dad Center.

1924: At the Olympic Games in Paris, the Duke, now thirty-four, wins the silver medal in the 100-meter freestyle. He is beaten for the first time by Johnny Weismuller. Copping the bronze medal that year is Duke's younger beachboy brother, Sam Kahanamoku.

1926: Swimmer-surfer Tom Blake, a Waikiki waterman who was originally from Wisconsin, accidently invents the hollow surfboard. Blake is trying to replicate a sixteen-foot board, a museum piece, when he begins drilling his board full of holes. After sealing the holes, Blake finds that he has created a lighter, longer surfboard that is well suited for paddleboard racing. His discovery revolutionizes surfboard design. In 1935, Blake will put the first skeg on a surfboard. That same year, he will test the first sailboard in the waters off Waikiki.

Circa 1929: A new sport, surf polo, is created at Waikiki by the Kahanamoku family. Patterned after water polo but played on a surfboard, the game is conducted in shallow water in front of the Royal Hawaiian Hotel. Among those competing are Duke and his brothers, Tom Blake, Buster and Buddy Crabbe, and a number of beachboys.

1932: Buster Crabbe is recognized as one of the world's fastest swimmers, winning the 400-meter freestyle at the Los Angeles Olympics. Crabbe, a future star of the silver screen, is one thirty-second Hawaiian. Most of his youth was spent in the islands, where he honed his skills as a waterman at Waikiki. Is he a beachboy? Not exactly, but he is known to have hustled surfing lessons at Waikiki and to have dived for coins in Honolulu Harbor.

1933: A major interisland canoe regatta—the first in a series of four—is established at Napoopoo on

In 1935, waterman-inventor Blake tested the first sailboard in the waters off Waikiki. From the Hawaii State Archives.

Two of Hawaii's greatest watermen, George Downing (foreground) and Wally Froiseth, once worked professionally as Waikiki beachboys. Photo courtesy of Wally Froiseth.

the island of Hawaii by, among others, Duke and David Kahanamoku, Dad Center, and professional beachboys John D. Kaupiko and Charlie Amalu. This is the first modern-day regatta organized exclusively for canoes. In its second year the event, again held at Napoopoo, draws twenty thousand spectators.

1938: Gene ("Tarzan") Smith, a twenty-six-year-old Waikiki beachboy, crosses the Molokai Channel on a thirteen-foot paddleboard—a first. Smith takes the shorter twenty-mile route between the two islands, landing at Makapuu Point on Oahu after being in the water for almost nine hours. In 1941, Smith will paddle the one hundred-mile channel connecting Oahu and Kauai. And in 1945 he will cross the forty-mile channel between Hawaii and Maui, thus realizing his ambition of paddling the Hawaiian Island chain on a surfboard.

Circa 1939: Wally Froiseth and a group of friends that includes his brother Jean, John Kelly, Gene Smith, Fran Heath, and later Duke Kahanamoku become the first in modern times to tackle the big winter surf at Sunset Beach and Makaha on Oahu's North and West shores. After the war they are joined by Woody Brown, George Downing, Rabbit Kekai, Blue Makua, Sr., and others. This coterie of Waikiki watermen are well-known adventure freaks. Brown's background is as a glider pilot. He had in 1938 just broken the world's distance record with a 263-mile flight from Wichita Falls, Texas, to Wichita, Kansas. John Kelly, who as a youth, witnessed an unsuccessful attempt by a crew of beachboys to ride twenty-foot Castle's Surf in an outrigger canoe, helps to train the Navy's first frogmen during the Second World War and earns a medal for going down sixty-eight feet and putting a shackle on a live torpedo.

1948: Woody Brown and his friend Alfred Kumalae design and build the original catamaran at Waikiki. When finished, the twin-hulled boat rides the breakers like a surfboard. It is the fastest thing in Hawaiian waters, with an estimated speed of twenty knots. Brown predicts it will not be long before he makes the first trans-Pacific crossing in a catamaran. That crossing comes seven years later, in 1955.

1952: Outrigger Canoe Club member A.E. ("Toots") Minvielle stages the first forty-mile, Molokai-to-Oahu canoe race. At the time, the idea of crossing the Molokai Channel, a hazardous stretch of water, is widely thought to be crazy. Nevertheless, the first race is completed without incident. In the years that follow, the event becomes the most prestigious open-ocean race of its kind in the world. Many of its most noted steersmen are Waikiki beachboys. Included among them are Blue Makua, Sr., Rabbit Kekai, Steamboat Mokuahi, Mud Werner, Blackout Whaley, and Alex Apo.

1954: Froiseth helps to organize the Makaha Surfing Championships, soon to become one of the world's top surfing events. Among the first winners are a number of Waikiki watermen and beachboys, including George Downing, Rabbit and Jama Kekai, and Froiseth himself.

Accounts of beachboy exploits also mention a number of more subtle skills. According to Wally Froiseth and Woody Brown, the beachboys could look at the ocean and determine when to go with the nets and when to go diving. They could look at the water and determine what the surf was going to be like the next day. The beachboys knew the tides, the winds, the currents. They could read the weather. They knew the different types of *limu* ("seaweed") and where to find them, and the names of the different kinds of fish and the various techniques for catching them. Some fish were attracted to smells and could be lured by throwing chewed coconut or crabmeat out on the water. Other fish were sensitive to sound and could be attracted by knocking together underwater two spears or a pair of rocks.

"All the beachboys had terrific breath," Froiseth recalled. "Blue could stay down three or four minutes, at least." Steamboat had what is commonly referred to as "squid eye," the ability while diving to look at a coral reef and know which holes contain squid.

"You'd look and say, 'I don't see a squid,'" said Froiseth. "Steamboat would say, 'Right there, you dummy.' 'Where?' You had to know what to look for. Any little change in color or movement, a little hole with white sand around it, or shells kicked out from the thing, that's a squid hole."

"Steamboat used to tell us," Froiseth continued, "that every fish has certain habits. *Uhu* eats certain types of coral. *Kumu* stays in a certain area. Turtles like to bed down in that crumbly finger coral. When Steamboat saw that you really wanted to learn, he'd take you out. Hell, it was an honor to go with him. George Downing and I used to watch him like a hawk. We knew we're going to learn something."

Almost all beachboys were expert fishermen. John ("Squeeze") Kamana, who was primarily known as a beachboy musician, went fishing every morning. At 6 A.M., he would run from his house on Kapahulu Avenue down to Queen's Surf, equipped with a two-foot, gum-rubber sling and an eight-foot spear. By 8:30 A.M., he would be coming home with a squid over his shoulder. It was Squeeze's practice to swim from Queen's Surf out toward Diamond Head, then across toward the Royal Hawaiian Hotel, and back to Queen's Surf, criss-crossing Waikiki so that no one ever knew exactly where it was that he caught his squid.

"My Dad was smart, they were all smart," recalled his son, Squeeze, Jr. "They would never show you where they went, what they did, how they did it. You'd have to watch and learn. When I was a kid the best fisherman on the beach was a guy named Peter Makia. He'd paddle over to where Kuhio Beach is, drift back, go around. Finally, he'd come back to the right of Canoe's, just off the Moana Hotel. He'd pull out his can of shrimp and throw the shrimp on top the water. The fish would all come up and—pow!—he'd throw the net one time and scoop up the fish. Then he'd paddle over by the Halekulani Hotel and park the canoe. He'd start cleaning the fish and tell us to go pick the *elele limu* ["black seaweed"] off the rock. When he was *pau* ["through"] cleaning, he'd put the fish in a bag and the limu on top the fish. When he came in everybody would run up and say, 'Eh, Makia, what you went catch?' He'd say, 'No catch nothing.'

In 1945, Waikiki beach-boy Gene "Tarzan" Smith became the first man to have paddled a surfboard across all of the channels connecting the major Hawaiian Islands. Photo 1938, from the Hawaii State Archives.

The first Molokai-to-Oahu canoe race, in 1952. The Waikiki Surf Club, pictured here, was one of only three crews competing in the forty-mile open ocean race. Crew members were, from left: George Downing, Roy Folk, Dutchie Kino, Moki Perkins, George Cabral, and Wally Froiseth. Photo courtesy of Wally Froiseth.

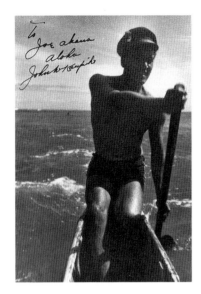

Bad day.' And he'd open his bag and show'em. 'We just went pick limu.'"

If beachboys were somewhat guarded about their practices, it was because they had to be; many made their living as fishermen when it was off-season for tourists. Much of their knowledge was the result of intense observation. "They watched what these fish were doing because they didn't want them to get away," Froiseth recalled. Then again, much of their knowledge was acquired from their elders. Lukela ("Old Man John D.") Kaupiko, for instance, had a talent for spotting fish in the water at great distances, a talent he no doubt acquired as a young boy on the island of Hawaii. Old Man John D. was born in Kapua on the Kona Coast, next to Milolii, an ancient Hawaiian fishing village which was—and still is—one of the last enclaves of the old ways.

Old Man John D., who moved to Waikiki in his early teens, inherited a sizable fortune. He was an heir to the Kanoa Estates, which had large landholdings on the island of Kauai, including the legendary Menehune Fishponds. He inherited beachfront property at Kapua, owned land in Waikiki, and eventually acquired a beautiful country house in Kailua on the windward side of Oahu. He was called "John D." after John D. Rockefeller.

"My grandfather was a good friend of the Dillingham family that lived out at Diamond Head Beach, and they used to allow him to use their property," recalled his grandson, *young* John D. Kaupiko.* "He'd go out there every evening and sit and look for fish, the mullet. I used to go out there with him when I was a young boy. We'd be sitting out there and all of sudden he'd yell, 'Quick, grab the net!' I'd grab the net. 'Hurry, run out there!' I'd start running. I'm going out on the reef and maybe it's knee-deep and I can't see the fish. 'Your left, go to your left!' I'd start moving to my left. Finally, a swell would be coming in and he'd yell, 'Throw! Throw the net!' And I'd just throw the net. When I picked it up, I'd have about fifty mullet. But I could never do that. I could never see the fish. I'd sit and look out at the ocean. But I could never see."

During his early years in Waikiki, Old Man John D. was Dude Miller's right-hand man on the beach; eventually, he took over his concession and for many years was Waikiki's head beachboy. Along with Duke Kahanamoku and Dad Center, he became an honorary member of the Outrigger Canoe Club. His most enduring accomplishment, however, was his success in coaching the Hui Nalu crew.

Legend has it that Old Man John D. could turn a canoe around a flag by just using his hips. Kaupiko was a master of the wicked hula; he had that certain motion in his hips, which he also used to his advantage in a canoe. "You sit in the back of the canoe and instead of using your paddle to *une*, or turn, you wiggle your *okole*," said Rabbit, winking. "Old Man John D. was the master of that move."

Old Man John D. Kaupiko led Hui Nalu to many championship seasons. As a coach he was known to love kids as much as he loved canoeing—but he was a tough taskmaster. After a long training run, he never let his crew ride a wave into the beach. When he felt a swell under the canoe, he made a certain

Old Man John D. Kaupiko, legendary beachboy canoe steersman and coach of the Hui Nalu crew. Photo courtesy of Joe Akana.

* There are three generations of Kaupikos: Lukela, or "Old Man John D." Kaupiko, John Kaupiko (with no "D."), and John D. Kaupiko, who was called *young* John D. to distinguish him from the others.

move with his paddle and took the canoe off the wave. His crew, after a moment of elation, suddenly found themselves dead in the water. He was teaching them to work, not to depend on the wave.

His students, who included Rabbit Kekai, Blue Makua, Sr., and Steamboat Mokuahi, were among the best steersmen on the beach—and the most durable. Rabbit was a repeat winner in the Molokai race and competed in or coached more than twenty. He remembered that one year before leaving for Molokai he told John D. he would be home for lunch. "When our canoe hit shore, it was 12:05. Old Man John D. came up to me afterward and said, 'You're late, Rabbit.'"

The most remarkable competitive record in the Molokai-to-Oahu race was compiled by Blue Makua, Sr. Between 1958 and 1963, he steered the Waikiki Surf Club to six straight championships, and in eleven races from 1953 through 1963, he was a member of eight winning teams. When he won in 1958, the newspapers reported that waves reached heights of fifteen feet and badly damaged two canoes, one of which split on one side. Conditions in 1961, according to the newspapers, were worse: high winds, occasional twenty-foot swells, and blinding rain squalls.

The *Honolulu Advertiser* reported that when Blue, Sr., sighted Koko Head Crater on Oahu's South Shore that year, the Waikiki Surf Club was in a neck-and-neck battle with the Lanikai Canoe Club. In a bit of skillful maneuvering, Blue, Sr., let the Lanikai team take the lead. The Lanikai canoe, however, soon hit fighting, or cross, currents. Calling for three fresh crewmen from his convoy boat, Blue, Sr., then steered straight for shore, "seemingly giving away the race." But when his canoe was about a hundred yards from shore, "they caught a Honolulu-bound current that swept them around the point and into a half-mile lead that they maintained to the finish." Skipper Guy Rothwell, of the escort boat *Mele*, who had convoyed in all ten previous races, called it the "most amazing bit of maneuvering" he had seen in the history of the event.

What does it take to be a great canoe steersman? According to Tommy Holmes, it takes an extensive knowledge of the ocean and waves. "In canoe surfing you've got to be able to size up that swell long before it ever gets to you, because you've got to start paddling long before it ever gets to you. Judgment, in a word, is one very important thing. Two, it takes a certain amount of brute strength. There's a certain amount of leverage involved. Third, you have to anticipate. Where does the anticipation come from? It comes from the seat of your pants. You can just feel it. It's an undefinable quality, like smelling the wind, a communion with the ocean that is so subtle and yet so profound."

Blue Makua, Sr., was said to have great anticipation, great feel. He could make a canoe slide through the surf like an eel. Steamboat had great strength. His chest was said to be as big around as a "beer keg," his canoe rides "as smooth as a Cadillac." Turkey Love had great judgment. "When I was doing it, I could spot

Surfboard polo was invented at Waikiki in 1929 by the Kahanamoku brothers. The sport was similar to water polo, except that it was played on surfboards. From the Hawaii State Archives.

a swell a half-mile out," he recalled. "I don't know how I could see the damn thing, but I could see it. I can't explain it. You have to know where to wait for it. You have to paddle a boat against the wind so that you can stay in that spot."

The same talents that made beachboys good canoe steersmen also made many of them gifted surfers. Excellent steersmen such as Duke and Sam Kahanamoku, Dad Center, George Downing, Rabbit Kekai, Blue Makua, Sr., Blackout Whaley, and Mud Werner were also, as one beachboy put it, "Lords of the Surf." They had a sixth sense. "If they were out in the water," the beachboy recalled, "and they were moving, you knew, just for survival purposes, they were moving for a reason. Like we're way outside, Castle's Surf, so far out we're in what's called Steamer Lane. The waves are so big you think they're going to cover the whole island. When the sets come in, it's like 'Stairways to the Heavens.' When those guys went after a wave, they got it. They knew that wave would wipe their ass out if they didn't. And they tried to ride that wave all the way into the beach. That was the ultimate."

Legend has it that one morning in 1917, following a great earthquake that originated in Japan, Duke and Dad Center woke up to the sight of huge surf off Diamond Head. That day they paddled out and recorded the longest rides on the biggest waves yet attempted: Castle's Surf, it was estimated, was thirty-feet high. Center's ride took him all the way to Cunha Break, a distance of three-quarters of a mile; Duke reportedly made it to shore, a distance of a mile and a quarter. Whether he really made it that far and whether the waves were really that big seem doubtful, however.[*] Froiseth, for one, pointed out that the redwood planks they rode in those days would not have provided the maneuverability such a ride required.

But while there may never have been a perfect ride, a few were near perfect. In the mid-1950s Blue Makua, Sr., caught a fifteen-foot wave at Castle's Surf and, according to Turkey Love, "damn near rode it to shore." The fact that so few came close suggests two things: the difficulty of the feat and the infrequent occurrence of truly big surf. Waikiki is situated on Oahu's South Shore, where the best surfing is available during the summer months. During most years, a good south swell will run at five to eight feet. A sustained swell larger than ten feet is invariably the result of disturbances in the Southern Hemisphere—just as the big winter surf on Oahu's North Shore is the result of disturbances in the Aleutian archipelago.

Nowadays, talk of fifteen- to twenty-foot surf at Waikiki would provoke laughter. But before 1950, great ground swells apparently moved in from across the equator with greater frequency. Wally Froiseth recalled that twice during the 1930s the surf rose to heights of more than twenty feet, and Waikiki was "closed out" all the way from Diamond Head to Honolulu Harbor. In fact, a diary he kept during one such stretch in 1939 contains daily entries noting whether the surf was "(b)," "(h)," or "(m)"—big, huge, or monstrous.

Woody Brown remembered stories about men who tried to ride this surf. Unable to get into the water from the beach, they went beyond Diamond Head to the cliff at Black Point. After shaking hands, they threw their boards and then themselves into the water and paddled around to meet the waves. Alas, the waves proved to be unridable.

George Downing, Buzzy Trent, and Woody Brown take off on a twenty-foot wave at Makaha in the late 1940s. According to Froiseth, this photo brought a new surge of California surfers to Hawaii. From the Hawaii State Archives. (Opposite page) Waikiki watermen and beachboys were among the first in modern times to test the big surf on Oahu's West and North shores. At Makaha Beach in 1949, from left: Russ Takaki, Rabbit Kekai, and Wally Froiseth. Roy Folk is seated in Froiseth's Phaeton V8 Ford. Photo courtesy of Wally Froiseth.

---

[*] Measuring the size of the wave is done from the back of the wave and is an inexact science. It is often said that oldtime surfers may have overestimated the size of waves while the reverse tends to be true of modern-day surfers.

Truth to tell, most beachboys were not big-wave riders. They were exhibitionists, their giant surfboards their stage. It was far more common to see a beachboy on a *small* wave, riding in while standing on his head, or carrying a woman in his arms, much as he might carry her across a threshold. The old-style surfboards were well suited for such antics. They were as big as beds—at least ten feet in length and well over a hundred pounds. Just carrying such a board took enormous strength. To ease the strain, a beachboy would shoulder it like a rifle. From the beach, he would run into the water and drop the board, jump on standing up, and glide out into the surf.

Buffalo Keaulana, the 1960 Makaha surfing champion who started his own contest—Buffalo's Big Board Classic—to revive the dying art of long-board surfing, explained that a basic difference between riding the big boards of yesterday and the smaller boards of today is that "on a small board, you make the board perform. On a big board, *you* perform."

On a big board it was possible to sit or lie down, carry a standing girl on your shoulders, to stand on one foot or face backwards, to do spinners or walk the board. A surfer could improvise endlessly—and many did. But few were better than Scooter Boy Kaopuiki. Even his nickname was derived from one of his many tricks: peddling his board with his foot to catch a wave.

When beachboys talk about Scooter Boy, they have trouble finding words to describe him adequately. Coming up short in mid-sentence, they will suddenly jump on a picnic table or begin running up and down their living-room floors, demonstrating how Scooter Boy rode his fifteen-foot hollow board. "Scooter Boy had that board flying all over the wave," said Buffalo as he snapped into his surfer's stance one day at Makaha Beach. "He would run to the front of the board, jump up in the air, and land on the nose, kicking the water from the nose so that the board would spin right around. And then he'd run to the back of the board. He was really a classic surfer."

"For sheer skill, natural know-how, and athletic talent, the guy was fabulous," said Wally Froiseth. "He did whatever he felt like doing, whenever he felt like doing it. That's how all the beachboys were. They wanted that free feeling, that free type of ocean living. Surfing was the expression of a lifestyle."

Scooter Boy was eight years old when he began surfing at Waikiki. The call of the ocean was like a siren, and it led quickly to expulsion from the Kamehameha School for Boys. Like so many other boys, Scooter Boy realized early on that the beach was his classroom. There were so many things to do at the beach, so many things to learn. There was a camaraderie there that was different, a camaraderie you could not find in a park or on a street corner. The older beachboys looked after you. Duke and the others started you surfing at Queen's and Canoe's and guided you to the more difficult breaks when you were ready. Old Man John D. steered you away from trouble and toward a canoe. There was a certain code that was observed on the beach. You learned to keep the beach clean, and as a result you felt clean. There was a respect for the ocean. When you went to the ocean, you took from it only what you needed. When you were a beachboy, the ocean was your mother. The beach was your life.

Duke Kahanamoku carries young Marston Campbell on his shoulders in surf off the Outrigger Canoe Club in 1910. Photo by A.R. Gurrey, from the Baker-Van Dyke Collection.

Duke Kahanamoku emerging from the surf at Waikiki, showing off the physique that earned him the title, the "Bronze Duke." Photo courtesy of Kimo Wilder McVay; hand-colored by Ron Hudson.

DUKE KAHANAMOKU
King of the Beach

3

I have never seen snow and do not know what winter means. I have never coasted down a hill of frozen rain, but every day of the year where the water is 76, day and night, and the waves roll high, I take my sled, without runners, and coast down the face of the big waves that roll in at Waikiki. How would you like to stand like a god before the crest of a monster billow, always rushing to the bottom of a hill and never reaching its base, and to come rushing in for half a mile at express speed, in graceful attitude, of course, until you reach the beach and step easily from the wave to the strand?

—Duke Kahanamoku

They called him the "Bronze Duke." He was, in fact, the king of the beach at Waikiki. During the first half of this century, he emerged as the world's consummate waterman, its fastest swimmer and foremost surfer, the first truly famous beachboy.

History remembers him as a transitional figure: the classic example of how men, places, and events often intersect at precisely the right moment. For Duke Paoa Kahanamoku that moment was August 11, 1911. In the still, glassy waters of Honolulu Harbor, at age twenty-one, he swam the 100-yard freestyle 4.6 seconds faster than anyone had before him.

In the course of the next twenty years he continued to defy time, competing in four Olympic Games and winning five medals. When he finally retired, at age forty-two, he could still swim as fast as when he was twenty-one.

He was the first man to surf on both the east and west coasts of the United States, as well as the first man to take surfing to Australia. He is credited with introducing surfing—and Hawaii—to the world. Who had ever heard of Waikiki before Duke? And what was a beachboy?

At that time, Hawaii was the last outpost of the United States. It was the most isolated spot on earth, farther away from any place than any other place in the world. And then along came Duke, shoring up that distance with a single, powerful swimming stroke, emerging onto the world stage as if he had just stepped off his surfboard.

The world was ready for Duke's arrival. But was Duke ready for the world? After the rush of Olympic fame had subsided, he discovered that he could not go back to the carefree existence of a Waikiki beachboy. Success demanded something more. He was forced to lead two lives: one in and one out of the water. "Out of the water I am nothing," he once said, lamenting that fact. He had trouble finding a suitable job. Between Olympic triumphs, he carved out an acting career in Hollywood; later, he was elected sheriff of Honolulu, then appointed to be the city's official greeter. But in Hollywood he was not really an actor—he was an extra, and the positions he held as sheriff and official greeter were largely honorary. In the end, fame never brought Duke much money, only ulcers.

But in the water he was different. Duke was the "human fish" and the "father of surfing." His name became synonymous with Waikiki and with the word "beachboy." People everywhere imagined all beachboys to look like Duke. His fame elevated the status of all beachboys. His celebrity contributed to their celebrity.

And yet in a professional sense, Duke was not a beachboy at all. "Duke was not in the business of being a beachboy," recalled former international surfing champion Fred Hemmings. "But in the larger sense of the word—of a man who lived and loved the ocean lifestyle—Duke was, as far as I'm concerned, the ultimate beachboy."

As a young man, Duke was a popular subject among island photographers, including Ray Jerome Baker, who snapped this shot in 1912. From the Baker-Van Dyke Collection. (Opposite page) Duke's trophy collection as it appeared in August, 1913, a year after he won his first Olympic gold medal at the age of twenty-two. From the L. E. Edgeworth Collection, courtesy of the Bernice Pauahi Bishop Museum.

Mother used to tell her children, "Go out as far as you want. Never be afraid in the water."

—Sargent Kahanamoku

From the beginning, Duke was a child of the sea. Born in 1890, he was among the last of the old Hawaiians, raised next to the ocean at Waikiki. One day as a small boy his father and uncle took him out in an outrigger canoe and threw him into the surf. "It was swim or else," Duke later recalled. "That's the way the old Hawaiians did it."

He attended Waikiki Grammar School, which was located directly across from the beach. In the afternoon, when the bell signaled the end of another school day, the children poured out of the classroom and headed toward the water. For Duke, it was a short trip from the chalkboard to the surfboard. He had five brothers—Sam, Dave, Billy, Louis, and Sargent—and they too loved the ocean. "All we did was water, water, water," Louis recalled. "My family believes we come from the ocean. And that's where we're going back."

In his teens Duke dropped out of high school to become a beachboy, gathering daily with the other beachboys beneath a hau tree at Waikiki. Together they surfed, swam, repaired nets, shaped surfboards, and sang. Eventually, they formed Hui Nalu, or "Club of the Waves," with Duke as their leader. The best waterman among them, he was a kind of spiritual leader. He did not drink. He did not smoke. He never fought unless provoked, and even then he did not punch, he slapped. He seldom raised his voice. Instead, he spoke with his eyes.

Years of rough-water swimming and canoe paddling molded Duke into a superb athlete. He had glistening white teeth, dark, shining eyes, and a black mane of hair that he liked to toss about in the surf. He stood six feet one and weighed 190 pounds. He had long, sinewy arms and powerful legs. He had the well-defined upper body that all great watermen possess, his "full-sail" shoulders tapering down to a slim waist and a torso that was "whipcord" tight.

And yet the most remarkable parts of Duke's body were his hands and feet. One veteran Outrigger Canoe Club member recalled that Duke's hands were so large that when he scooped up ocean water and threw it at you it looked like a whole bucket. "He could cradle water in his hands, cupping it between his palms, and just shoot a fountain at you. It came with great force. He would often cross his hands in the water—slapping the surface—and it would just be boom! boom!"

Legend has it that Duke could steer a canoe with his feet. "He had fins for feet," Rabbit Kekai recalled. "He didn't need a paddle." When he surfed, Duke could make a board without a skeg slide across the face of a wave, and when he swam, the famous "Kahanamoku kick" was so powerful that his body actually rose up out of the water—"like a speed boat with its prow up." His brother Sargent recalled the first time he saw Duke swim in a sanctioned meet. The site was the Waikiki Natatorium, a salt-water swimming pool situated on the flank of Diamond Head. The oldtimers told Sargent to watch his brother, that when he swam he created waves. That night Duke jumped in the water and started down the middle of the tank.

He went about twenty yards and, sure enough, the waves spread out and hit the sides. "And I mean they were big," said Sargent. So big, he said, it seemed as if he could have taken his surfboard and gone for a ride.

Duke's brother, Bill, recalled stories about how Duke often went for long swims at Waikiki, out beyond the reef into waters where there were sharks. Duke believed the shark was his *aumakua*, his guardian. "When he went to Australia to show them surfing," Bill said, "the lifeguards tried to stop him. They said, 'You can't go out there. There are a lot of man-eating sharks.' Duke said, 'Ah, no, I'll go out.' Hundreds of people lined the beach to watch. He paddled out, caught the waves, sliding right, sliding left. When he came in, the lifeguards asked him, 'Did you see any sharks?' Duke said, 'Yeah, I saw plenty.' 'And they didn't bother you?' the lifeguards asked. 'No, Duke replied, 'and I didn't bother them.'"

At Waikiki Duke was among the few who dared ride Castle's Surf. He had the biggest board, a sixteen footer made of solid koa that weighed 114 pounds. Big boards were for big waves, and when Duke caught one he'd yell, "Coming down!"

"Duke was never afraid of anything in the sea," recalled Kenneth Brown, a prominent part-Hawaiian who sailed the turbulent interisland channels with Duke. Often they traveled down to the Kona Coast of the island of Hawaii, where Brown had spent part of his youth. "Duke reminded me of many of the Hawaiians I had met there," he said. "Their sense of their environment was unusual. They didn't differentiate much between what was above and below the sea. They had place names for all the hills and bays like we do, but they also had place names for things *down* in the water. That's the way it was with Duke. The ocean was such a familiar, friendly environment for him. He was no more afraid of what might happen to him at sea than you or I would be of getting hit by a car crossing the street. The ocean was his home."

But Duke was as unfathomable out of the water as he was fearless in it. Joe Brennan, his biographer, wrote that Duke "seemed to live way down inside himself." To be sure, he was not a big talker. He had a mind that saw deeply and in detail, but he was very contained, reticent almost to a fault. Like the vast ocean itself, he seemed for the most part to exist below the surface.

Duke also favored traditional ways. He spoke Hawaiian. He preferred Hawaiian foods. He believed that canoes and surfboards should be made the old way. There is a story about a surfer nicknamed "Mongoose" who sharpened the rounded nose of his board so that he could cut easily left and right across the waves. Duke watched him from afar, and although he disapproved he said nothing. And then one day when the

Duke was king of the beach. Here he stands at the head of the line in a late 1920s portrait taken in front of the old Moana Pier. Photo by Ray Jerome Baker, from the Sawtelle-Van Dyke Collection.

board was left unattended, he picked it up, carted it away, and sawed off the nose.

Sammy Amalu, a notorious Hawaiian con man who later became a newspaper columnist and whose father, Charlie Amalu, was a well-known beachboy, once wrote that year in and year out Duke never changed. "The Duke was just the Duke," he stated. "Like Aloha Tower or Diamond Head or the beach at Waikiki, the Duke was always there. Just being himself. Just being the Duke."

"He had an inner tranquility," recalled Kenneth Brown. "It was as if he knew something we didn't know. He had a tremendous amount of simple integrity. Unassailable integrity. You rarely meet people who don't have some persona they assume to cope with things. But Duke was completely transparent. No phoniness. People could say to you that Duke was simple—the bugga must be dumb! No way. That's an easy way of explaining that. Duke was totally without guile. He knew a lot of things. He just knew 'em."

Was Duke a "dumb bugga?" His reticence often led people to that conclusion. Duke had his own answer to that question. "*Mahape a ale wala'au,*" he would say in Hawaiian. "Don't talk—keep it in your heart."

Both men of big, powerful, well-built bodies. Both skilled at all the favorite sports, but loving surfriding the best. Both conquering all the world there was to conquer. Kamehameha at war, Duke at swimming.
—**Tom Blake**

I t was perhaps inevitable that the world would discover such a unique talent. During the summer of 1911, Duke was taking one of his daily swims off Sans Souci Beach at Diamond Head when he was clocked in the 100-yard sprint by attorney William T. Rawlins, the man who was to become his first coach. At Rawlins' urging, Duke and his friends had founded Hui Nalu, then entered the first sanctioned Hawaiian Amateur Athletic Union swimming and diving championships which were held on August 11 at Honolulu Harbor. It was a memorable day, one that saw Hui Nalu sweep eleven events. Equally significant, Duke won the 100-yard freestyle event in the astonishing time of 55.4 seconds, shattering the world record held by U.S. Olympic champion Charles M. Daniels. As if that were not enough, he also equaled Daniels' world record time of 24.2 seconds in the 50-yard freestyle event.

Results of the meet were telegraphed to Amateur Athletic Union headquarters in New York, where officials reacted with utter disbelief. Never mind that the feat had been clocked by five certified judges. Or that the course had been measured four times, once by a professional surveyor. Upon learning that an unknown twenty-one-year-old Hawaiian had shattered the world's most important swimming record, on a course set up between two piers in a salt-water harbor, one Amateur Athletic Union official reportedly replied, "And what were you using for stopwatches—alarm clocks?"

Duke's record times were not recognized.*

* In disallowing his times, Amateur Athletic Union officials in New York reasoned that Duke must have been aided by strong currents in Honolulu Harbor. A study of the harbor several years later, after Duke had become a proven champion, revealed otherwise and his records were allowed.

Poised to dive, Duke shows the perfect form that made him the world's fastest swimmer for more than a decade. From the collection of Kaniau Evans.

Duke went back into training, determined to prove himself. With money raised by his Hui Nalu teammates, he was sent off to the Olympic tryouts in the winter of 1912. At a warm-up meet in Chicago, his first stop, Duke finished last when his legs cramped in the cold water. In Pittsburgh and New York, however, he recovered and won handily, making it to the finals of the Olympic trials in Philadelphia, where he qualified for the U.S. team by winning the 100-meter freestyle in a time of 60 seconds.

The crowds were entranced—as much by his physical presence as by his swimming prowess. According to his manager, Lew Henderson, "the ovation that greeted Duke in Philadelphia was nothing short of thunderous. He was clad in a nile-green swimming suit, over which had been wrapped an American flag, and this covered by a dark robe. When he appeared, the applause began....Withdrawing the robe and displaying the encircling flag heightened it, and finally the sight of his build was followed by a deafening round of cheers and yells."

A few weeks later in Verona Lake, New Jersey, Duke qualified as a member of the U.S. 800-meter relay team, swimming his 200-meter leg in a time of 2:40.0, six-tenths of a second faster than the existing world record held by Daniels. The swimming world was again shocked. As a sprint swimmer, Duke was not expected to excel at middle-distance events.

In New York, Duke boarded the boat for Stockholm, accompanied on his trans-Atlantic voyage by Jim Thorpe, the American Indian who would prove to be the hero of the 1912 Olympics. Thorpe dominated the track and field events, which were the primary focus of the games. Duke dominated swimming, which was still a minor Olympic sport, a circumstance sorely underscored by the condition of Stockholm's Olympic pool. With no starting blocks, no lane markers, and no visible bottom, it looked like a big, brown, open vat. Duke felt right at home; he said it reminded him of Honolulu Harbor.

He breezed through the preliminaries—in one heat bettering by three seconds Daniels' Olympic record for the 100-meter freestyle. In preparation for the finals, he marked both ends of the pool with a towel, a tactic he devised to help him stay in his own lane. That done, he won the gold easily, actually slowing at the finish when he craned his head back to see how far ahead he was. Sweden's King Gustaf summoned him to the royal victory stand. As Duke stood humbly silent before the king, the stadium stood and cheered.

In the aftermath of his victory, Duke went on a swimming tour of Europe. Wherever he went, his name was often mistaken for a title. Was the Duke really a duke? Or perhaps even a king? The European press began to probe, looking for a royal connection. Duke just shrugged. As far as he knew, he was just "a beachboy from Waikiki."

Back in Honolulu, historians and others who were interested in Duke's genealogical lines established that his ancestors were related by blood to Bernice Pauahi Paki Bishop—"the last of the Kamehamehas." So it was true. Duke was related to royalty, to Kamehameha the Great himself.

King Gustaf of Sweden joins in the applause after awarding Duke the gold medal for winning the 100-meter freestyle at the 1912 Olympic Games. Photo courtesy of Kimo Wilder McVay.

Duke occupied a status he never aspired to. Thank God he was elected sheriff and given the job of official greeter, because if he would have had to earn a living, he would have starved. Out of the water, he was out of his element.

—George ("Airedale") McPherson

Duke returned home a conquering hero, but there was inside him a growing sense of insecurity. Here he was, twenty-two years old, and the only thing he knew was the ocean. After the celebration came to an end, he had to ask himself: what am I returning home to?

What was he going to do? Was it time for him to climb out of the pool, put on a business suit, and go to work? Duke tried. He tried being a water-meter reader. He tried working in the drafting department of the Territorial government. He tried being a surveyor. On and off for many years, he even tried being a beachboy, only to find there was not much money or dignity in it for a man of his stature.

He began accepting invitations to compete abroad in exhibition swimming meets. Travel cleared his mind and kept him active. More important, it kept him in the water. Wherever possible, Duke combined a swimming exhibition with a demonstration of the sport of surfing. On his trip to Australia in 1915, he fashioned a board out of sugar pine, and on a day when the seas were running high at Freshwater Beach, he provided the Aussies with a spectacular three-hour show that marked the real beginning of the sport Down Under. In 1916, he promoted surfing on the east coast of the United States with demonstrations at Atlantic City, New Jersey, and Nassau, New York. The First World War resulted in the cancellation of the Olympic Games, so Duke went on tour for the Red Cross, raising money with other American aquatic champions to aid its efforts during the war.

In 1920, at age thirty, Duke successfully defended his title as the world's fastest swimmer at the Antwerp Olympics. (It was not until the 1924 Paris Olympics that he was defeated by Johnny Weismuller, an occurrence that allowed him in later years to joke that "it took Tarzan to beat me.") Again, he returned home to a king's welcome. Again, he was forced to contemplate his future out of the water. And again, he began receiving offers—this time from Hollywood. On and off for four decades, Duke played bit parts in twenty-eight films. Typically, he was cast in brown-skin roles—an Indian chief, a Hindu thief, an Arab prince—but rarely as a Hawaiian and rarely in his element. In fact, during the first five years he was under contract he never got his feet wet.

His finest moment in Hollywood took place off stage. One June day in 1925 at Newport Beach, Duke was enjoying a picnic with fellow actors when a pleasure yacht, the *Thelma*, capsized in raging offshore surf. Of the twenty-nine people on board that day, seventeen died. With his surfboard, Duke managed to save eight, thrice battling his way out and back through churning white water. Newport's police chief called Duke's performance "the most superhuman surfboard rescue act the world has ever seen," but when it was over Duke did not wait around to be thanked. He simply left.

In 1929, he left Hollywood and returned to Hawaii where, approaching forty, his prospects for a career

Off and on for four decades, Duke played bit parts in twenty-eight Hollywood films. The names of many of those films have been forgotten, but not their stars. Above, Duke with Wallace Beery, and (opposite page) with Ronald Coleman. Photos courtesy of Kimo Wilder McVay.

were no better than they had been when he was younger. He accepted a job as the superintendent of City Hall, but he later found out that he was in fact only a glorified janitor. A newspaper reported that Duke could be seen mowing the lawn during the afternoon rush hour. "This is the best time to show I am working," Duke was quoted as saying. "Everybody passes along here around this time and they all see me earning my salary." Next, he opened a pair of gas stations. A song written about the new venture was entitled "Duke Kahanamoku, Former Olympic Champion, Now Pumping Gas."

Illness had forced Duke to miss the 1928 Olympics, but in 1932, at age forty-two, he went to Los Angeles for his last attempt to make the U.S. Olympic swim team. Although he failed, he did manage to qualify as a member of the water polo team. In an amazing replay of his former glory, he swam the 100-meter freestyle in a trial meet in 59.8 seconds, a time that bettered his winning performance at the 1912 Olympics.

Returning to Honolulu again, Duke decided to turn his fame into political advantage and ran for the office of sheriff. He was a shoo-in candidate, elected to thirteen consecutive two-year terms—often without campaigning and more than once while he was not even in the Territory of Hawaii. Being sheriff required him to run the jail, issue summonses, and act as coroner, but for the most part the job was honorary and paid little.

After a day at the sheriff's office, Duke headed for the beach. He rode the surf when it was up, went for long swims when it was not, and played surfboard polo and volleyball at the Outrigger Canoe Club. Duke was forever breaking records for athletic longevity. Up until he was fifty, he remained a big-wave surfer, and up until 1950, when he turned sixty, he was Waikiki's best canoe steersman. During the 1940s, he guided the Outrigger Canoe Club to seven straight championship seasons. "Even when his physical ability started to wane because of age, he excelled because of his knowledge of the ocean and what he was doing," Fred Hemmings recalled. "I'd watch him surfing when he was older. He was always at the right place at the right time. He always caught the good wave."

Long before his days as a competitive athlete were over, Duke stepped gracefully into the role of being Hawaii's unofficial ambassador. Whenever there was a famous person in town—a movie star, a king, or the President—Duke would always take him for an outrigger canoe ride. Yet for all the apparent ease with which he handled the job, few men were more uncomfortable in the limelight. In 1950, Duke traveled to New York with beachboys Chick Daniels and Splash Lyons to appear on Arthur Godfrey's radio and television programs. Before the first show Duke grew apprehensive. "Chick can dance," he said. "And Splash can sing and play ukulele. But what am I going to do?"

After he left Hollywood in 1929, Duke returned to Hawaii and struggled to find a suitable job. At one point, he opened a pair of gas stations. Soon after, a song was written about his new venture entitled, "Duke Kahanamoku, Former Olympic Champion, Now Pumping Gas." Photo courtesy of Barbara Kahanamoku Robello.

Duke seemed to become a hostage of his own celebrity, and some say it eventually contributed to his physical decline. In 1955, he survived a heart attack. Within the next decade, he re-entered the hospital for gastric ulcers, the removal of a blood clot in his brain, and a prostate operation. Equally worrisome was his financial health. At its best Duke's job as sheriff paid him less than $10,000 a year. Business ventures, such as a line of aloha shirts bearing his name, always seemed to make money for others but not for Duke. In 1961, Arthur Godfrey made a plea on Duke's behalf, saying that except for his home he owned nothing. In a rare public outburst, Duke said that he had spent his life promoting Hawaii. "And what have I got to show for it?" he asked. "Nothing. And I'm not going to ask for anything." Said his brother Louis, "A lot of people took my brother for a ride. Duke was easy. Too goddamn easy."

How could a man who was so adept in the water be so inept out of it? And did it really bother him? Was there anyone to blame? Those closest to Duke did not escape criticism. Some said that his brothers had traded on the Kahanamoku name, and while it is true that they never tried to downplay the fact that they were related to him, all were quite accomplished in their own right.

Even Duke's wife of twenty-eight years came under attack. Nadine Alexander was a worldly and sophisticated dance instructor at the Royal Hawaiian Hotel when Duke married her in 1940. At the time he proposed, he told her that she would be marrying a poor man. Later she confessed, "I didn't know then how poor he really was." There are those who say that it was she who stirred up resentment over his financial woes, but perhaps she was justified in doing so. It was tragic that Duke, in the sunset of his life, was still running in place on a financial treadmill.

Kimo Wilder McVay, Duke's personal manager during his last eight years, was also viewed with suspicion. McVay was an enterprising island disc jockey whose mother, Kinau, had as a child been taught by Duke to swim. One day in 1959 he was interviewing Duke when he remarked that he had seen an ad for his shirts in a national magazine.

"You must make a lot of money from that, Duke," McVay said. "Those shirts are sold in the best stores all over the country."

"Well, Kimo, I only made ninety-seven dollars last year," Duke replied.

"How is that possible? Will you let me look into that?"

The result was the creation of Duke Kahanamoku Enterprises, which was managed by McVay and financed by his mother. The three of them joined forces around 1961, about the same time the city abolished the office of sheriff and made Duke the official greeter.

As the city's official greeter, Duke met the Queen Mother of England when she stopped over at the Honolulu International Airport in 1966. At Duke's left is his wife Nadine. To the left of the Queen Mother is former Hawaii Governor John A. Burns. Photo courtesy of Kimo Wilder McVay.

McVay immediately set to work repairing Duke's tarnished image. In 1962, when President John F. Kennedy came to Hawaii, Duke, the city's official greeter, was not invited to meet him at the airport. McVay got a columnist to drop an item in the newspaper: "Surely the Duke is going to be there?" And, of course, he was immediately invited. "I went to the airport with him, with the Lieutenant Governor," McVay recalled. "And I'm in the back watching this. There are all the officials of the Senate, the Governor, and way at the end of the receiving line is Duke, in his white outfit. Out comes Kennedy. He goes down the receiving line: 'Hello, hello, hello.' Suddenly, he gets to Duke and stops. You can see the lights and cameras going on and the flashbulbs popping. He spends about five minutes with Duke—and to think he wasn't even going to be there!"

McVay was everything that Duke was not—shrewd, glib, outgoing. He was also an ingenious promoter. He recast Duke as a king in white and outfitted him in all the trappings of royalty. He bought him a boat and a Rolls Royce with surfboard racks on the top. He put Duke's name on clothes, ukuleles, skateboards, and surfboards, and to help sell the surfboards he formed the Duke Kahanamoku surf team, which comprised four of the world's top surfers: Fred Hemmings, Paul Strauch, Jr., Joey Cabell, and Butch Van Artsdalen.

In 1966, McVay helped to inaugurate the Duke Kahanamoku Surfing Classic, which was filmed by CBS and nominated for an Emmy. According to McVay, however, not all of these promotions made money. The "mother lode" was the creation of Duke Kahanamoku's nightclub in Waikiki, to which McVay lured Don Ho, then a relatively unknown local singer, and made him a star.

McVay was often accused of profiting more than Duke from the partnership. Some family members say that he took both the car and the boat back after Duke died. Still, Duke's last years with McVay were among his best. He looked great, wanted for little, and was finally accorded the respect that was due him. When he was not traveling, he could usually be found down at the beach or on his boat. On Sunday evenings he held forth at his nightclub. He had the King's table. He was the King. "People say I exploited him," McVay recalled. "Ha! He loved it."

Were there a lot of people who took advantage of Duke? Duke's good friend, Kenneth Brown, offered a different perspective. "You might think so if you looked at it cynically," he said. "But you really couldn't take advantage of him. You really couldn't dent old Duke. I knew him when he was older. I know there were others around him who wanted him to be financially successful. But I never felt Duke had his heart in that. He was Duke. Duke was Duke. His values came from the sea. He walked through a Western world, but he was always essentially Hawaiian. And because of the simplicity and purity of that value system, money was never that important to him."

It was as if they were burying the last king of Hawaii. There were people everywhere, on every hotel balcony. But the most impressionable thing was the ocean. It was churning and storming and the old Hawaiian ladies were weeping, as if they were very aware that the forces of nature were affected.

—Fred Hemmings

Duke carried on his love affair with the ocean up until the end. The water was his lifestyle, his tonic, and he had to partake of it daily. One day in January of 1968 Duke was opening the trunk of his Rolls Royce in the parking lot of the Waikiki Yacht Club when he fell, striking his head first on the rear of his car and then on the pavement. His brother Bill discovered him moments later. One eye was closed and there was blood. Duke was dead. At age seventy-seven he had been struck down by a heart attack, and all Hawaii mourned. "There is a strange sound in the booming surf at Waikiki today," reported the *Star-Bulletin*, "like the anguished cry of a mother at the loss of her favorite son."

Two funeral services were scheduled for the following Saturday, a traditional church service with Arthur Godfrey delivering the eulogy, followed by a beachboy service at Waikiki. On the sand in front of the Royal Hawaiian, Duke's canoe lay waiting, his surfboard resting across it. Beachboys stood guard between the canoe and the water, each with his surfboard stuck in the sand behind him. In tribute they held a short ceremony, concluding with the song "Aloha Oe."

Sargent led a procession of canoes out to sea. The steering seat on the lead canoe was left empty, and propped up in the stern was Duke's paddle. "The canoes went out two abreast," Sargent later recalled in an interview, "and I planned to go out beyond the reef, where we would form our circle. But this is the part...I will never forget...we could not make that circle. It just seemed like we had hit a wall. All the canoes came to a dead stop in the water....brother Bill and I were amazed. Every man in the canoes was trying to paddle forward, but the canoes were not moving. I said to brother Bill, 'I guess this is the spot where he wants to be.' Reverend [Abraham] Akaka said his prayers right there where we were and that's where brother Duke was laid to rest.

"And it was interesting...that when we turned to paddle to shore, there was no racing—no yelling, no screaming. It was like everyone felt respect for the man we left behind. Later on, I saw a picture...and believe it or not [it was] a picture of a shark's fin cutting through the water near where brother Duke was dropped....Bill and I have often thought back to that day. Duke was never afraid of the blue water. Could this shark be an *aumakua* for brother Duke...there to guide him 'home'?"*

* Sargent told this story in 1984 in a taped interview with Kenneth Pratt of the Outrigger Canoe Club.

"It was as if they were burying the last king of Hawaii," is how one observer described Duke's 1968 beachboy funeral at Waikiki. The Reverend Abraham Akaka holds Duke's urn. Behind Akaka are Arthur Godfrey (in sunglasses) and Nadine Kahanamoku. Photo by Charles Okamura, courtesy of the *Honolulu Advertiser.*

THE KAHANAMOKU BROTHERS

The Duke stands between his sisters at the funeral of his mother, Julia Paoa Kahanamoku. At left are Duke's five brothers. Photo courtesy of Barbara Kahanamoku Robello. (Opposite page) The Kahanamoku brothers in front of the old Moana Bathhouse, circa 1928. From left: Bill, Sam, Louis, David, Sargent, and Duke. Photo by Tai Sing Loo, courtesy of the Bernice Pauahi Bishop Museum.

The eldest of nine children. Duke Kahanamoku had five brothers who, unlike himself, spent a good portion of their lives as Waikiki beachboys. Although none of the brothers became nearly as famous as Duke, all were similar in physique and appearance, and all could claim substantial talents.

Next to Duke, Sam was the most celebrated. A gifted swimmer, surfer, and canoeman, he captured the bronze medal in the 100-meter freestyle at the 1924 Paris Olympics. He was also a gifted singer; his rich baritone voice could be heard on Sunday evenings when the beachboys gathered on the old Moana Pier. He later became the caretaker of "Shangri-la," the seaside mansion owned by tobacco heiress Doris Duke.

Brother David, who later became a farmer on Maui, was a good enough swimmer to have made the 1924 Olympic swim team. In 1961, an Associated Press dispatch from Jones Beach, New York, reported that "an unusual combination of waves and undertow imperiled scores of swimmers Sunday at this resort center. Nine were pulled to safety by David Kahanamoku." At the time he made this daring rescue, David was sixty-seven years old.

Louis Kahanamoku, who became deputy sheriff under Duke, was a talented surfboard paddler, water-polo player, and canoe coach. Along with Sam and Sargent, he is credited with inventing surfboard polo, a game which became the rage at Waikiki during the late 1920s and 1930s.

Bill ("Tarball") Kahanamoku, the only brother to have a nickname, was a popular beachside comedian who worked for years as caretaker for Herb Briner, owner of Kahala Manufacturing and the yacht *Miss Hawaii*. Tarball, who also was the shortest of the six brothers, was distinguished by a crooked spine, while Sargent Kahanamoku, the youngest brother, had a long crooked nose. "Hey, Sarge, move your nose," the other beachboys would tease. "No can see Diamond Head."

Sargent, who later became the official greeter for Standard Oil Company in Hawaii, was a powerful swimmer. In the 100-meter freestyle, he was once clocked at under 60 seconds. In 1933, he made a famous rescue at Waikiki, single-handedly towing a disabled speed boat to shore and saving the life of Paul Fagan, president of Universal Motors.

According to a newspaper account, "the two had gone out for a spin when Fagan's boat ran out of gas about three-and-a-half miles off shore and started to drift. After trying vainly to make headway by paddling with a seat torn from the boat, Sargent jumped overboard and began to swim to shore, towing the craft. There was no rope available, so Sargent was forced to hang on to the bow with one hand and paddle with the other, kicking at the same time." Four hours later he made it to safety.

In addition to five brothers, Duke had three sisters: Bernice, Kapiolani, and Maria, the last of whom died in 1932 at age twenty-five. His father, Duke Halapu Kahanamoku, was a policeman whose birth in 1869 coincided with the first visit to the Islands of the Duke of Edinburgh. His mother, Julia Paoa, came from Kalia, the dry ewa end of Waikiki, which is today the site of the Hilton Hawaiian Village.

The beachboys were the inspiration for such songs as "Sunshine the Beachboy," with lyrics by R. Alex Anderson, one of Hawaii's most prolific and creative songwriters. From the Baker-Van Dyke Collection.

A BEACHBOY PARTY

Melody and Magic
on the Moana Pier

4

I care not for cafe life
for Waikiki is good enough for me
I care not for silks and lace
for a bathing suit is good enough for me
Society may be the fashion
but I crave simplicity....
I care not for squabs on toast
for fish and poi is good enough for me

—"Cafe Life,"
a beachboy song
performed on the old Moana Pier

ew Waikiki landmarks jut out into the memory like the old Moana Pier. Years ago the pier stood at the heart of the beach, reaching out some three hundred feet toward the reef. At the end of the pier there was a square pavilion. Here, on Sunday evenings, the beachboys came to play their music and sing their songs. People jammed the pavilion, lined the walkway, or sat along a seawall that ran toward Diamond Head. Others straddled surfboards in the water or gathered on rafts, the men drawing straws to determine who would bring out drinks from the beach.

The music began after it got dark, so softly at first that it seemed to be coming in off a wave. "You couldn't beat the music that came from the pier on Sunday nights," beachboy Joe Akana recalled. "What music! What voices! No more voices like that any more. And the songs! You won't hear those songs anywhere else."

The songs were delivered in elaborate harmonies. A choir of voices would rise in crescendo and stop, the sound of the surf punctuating the pause, and then start up softly again. "These Hawaiian beachboys seemed to weave a spell of the real Hawaii over the assemblage," composer Johnny Noble reminisced in a 1944 issue of *Paradise of the Pacific* magazine. "Tourists and local residents alike sat quietly while they listened, enchanted, to the island music that stirred the heart…. The boys had no set program, for it was all informal, but they would play and sing song after song, a surf of melody."

The beachboy musicians included Splash Lyons on ukulele and his brother, Freckles, on guitar; Hiram Anahu, a wonderful bass singer and the composer of such hits as "Drifting" and "All Because of You"; Joe Ikiole, a falsetto who played slack key; and baritones Joe Bishaw, Pua Kealoha, and Sam Kahanamoku. "We'd just sing and sing," remembered Sam's brother, Bill Kahanamoku. "And we weren't singing for the people. We were singing for ourselves. The people just came. Pretty soon they wanted the lights on. They wanted to see who was singing. We told the hotel, 'The moon is our spotlight. You put the lights on, we don't sing.'"

One evening the hotel approached Sam Kahanamoku and asked him if he would perform in the dining

Out in Honolulu where the palm trees grow
lives a sweet Hawaiian maiden that loves me so
And when the moon is softly shining
We tell our stories all night long
listening to the music of the surf's wild roar
as it beats upon the golden shore….
She is my Rose of Honolulu, she is my Hawaiian queen

room. Sam agreed, and that night after dinner he delivered an inspiring rendition of Tom Armstrong's "Rose of Honolulu." "Boy! He sang that song!" Bill recalled. "A lot of people were walking out—they didn't know who my brother was. But when they heard that voice, they all sat down. They all went crazy. They said, 'That's the voice that sings out on the pier!'"

Beachboy ukulele master Squeeze Kamana performs at a 1937 Shriner's convention in Los Angeles. Photo courtesy of Squeeze Kamana, Jr. (Opposite page) The Moana Hotel and Pier at night in 1919. Tourists and local residents alike once jammed onto the pier every Sunday evening to hear the beachboys play their music and sing their songs. Photo by Tai Sing Loo, courtesy of the Bernice Pauahi Bishop Museum.

PROPERTY OF : DAWN ANAHU FERNANDEZ
45-326 Kahiko Street
Kaneohe, HI 96744

When You Come Back

Featured by
KEAUMOKU LOUIS
Hawaiian Serenaders
Victor Record 26387

Words
and
Music
by
"HIRAM"
B. K. ANAHU

Published
by
Oscar U. Hyatt
HONOLULU, T.H.

"When You Come Back," one of many compositions by beachboy songwriter Hiram Anahu. Courtesy of Charlie Lambert.

The Moana Pier was condemned in 1930, but along the waterfront and throughout Waikiki, the music of the beach continued to find expression. Music was as much a part of the beachboy's life as the water. R. Alex Anderson, born in 1894 and one of Hawaii's most prolific and creative songwriters, recalled that "music was natural to the beachboys. It was a part of them. I think they were inspired by Waikiki, by the feeling the beach gives you of music. Most of them had a comic streak— laughing, joking, full of life."[*]

Few beachboys had any formal musical training. Sitting around on the beach they learned from each other, listening, watching, imitating. Each day when the canoes and surfboards were put away, the guitars and ukuleles appeared, and parties born of the moment, comprising equal parts of song and drink, carried on far into the night.

Parties could be found everywhere at Waikiki. They began aboard the luxury cruisers as they steamed into Honolulu Harbor, continued nightly in suites at the Moana and Royal Hawaiian hotels, at luaus, and at clubs like the Waikiki Tavern where the beach crowd congregated.

If an evening held no promise of a party, the beachboys might dress up and serenade along the beach or down Kalakaua Avenue and out toward Diamond Head. If they heard a party going on, they would wander over and start playing music on the lawn. They did this for two reasons: for the love of it and because they always got in on the party.

The reputations the beachboys had as bons vivants enhanced their mystique. Joe Akana, born in 1907 and something of a beachside historian, recalled that at thirteen he was already staying out all night drinking "swipes," or chilled pineapple mash, and playing ukulele with a group of beachboys who gathered along Waikiki's Diamond Head seawall. "We used to have parades," he said. "We got a big bass drum and marched to slack key. We'd march at night—Duke was our leader—and control the roads. People would toot their horns, but we wouldn't move."

Beachboys took their fun seriously, but their merrymaking tended to obscure the fact that they were also serious musicians—popular with residents, visitors, and royalty alike. Queen Liliuokalani, for instance, the last reigning Hawaiian monarch before annexation, was on hand with Princess Kalanianaole when the beachboys organized their famous 1914 fund raiser, the "Hui Nalu Follies," which was performed at the old Honolulu Opera House.

Prince Kuhio, Hawaii's delegate to Congress from 1902 to 1922, often conducted visitation parties to the Islands, entertaining U.S. House and Senate members whose support he was trying to enlist. Akana recalled that around 1920, when Kuhio was seeking passage of a bill that would create the Hawaiian Homes Commission, he threw a lavish luau at his Waikiki estate and called upon the beachboys to help

[*] R. Alex Anderson is the composer of more than one hundred hapa-haole songs, including "Lovely Hula Hands" and "Cockeyed Mayor of Kaunakakai." He married Peggy Center, sister of famed Honolulu waterman Dad Center.

with the entertainment.* Behind a seawall in his backyard, he erected bleachers and then constructed a stage some twenty to thirty feet out in the water. The beachboys suited up in *malos* and other Hawaiian garb, loaded their canoes with fruits and leis, and together with other entertainers, paddled out from the beach at nightfall, making a surprise entrance from the sea to a stage ringed by firelight.

The passage of the Hawaiian Homes Commission bill earned Prince Kuhio his place in history, but unfortunately the same cannot be said of the beachboys and their music. *Hawaiian Music and Musicians: An Illustrated History*, edited by George Kanahele, makes little reference to the beachboys as composers or musicians. Their contribution to the development of Hawaiian music was an indirect one. In the same way that jazz music and black music often took their inspiration from the streets, Hawaiian music often took its inspiration from the beach.

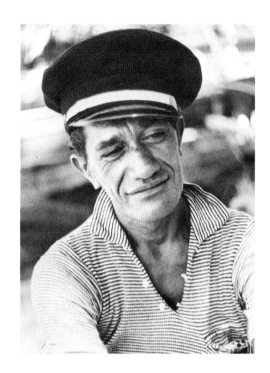

As an example, *hapa-haole* music (Hawaiian music given a Western tilt to make it more appealing to tourists) became a national craze when Albert ("Sonny") Cunha performed Henry Kailimai's "On the Beach at Waikiki" at the 1915 Panama-Pacific International Exhibition in San Francisco, an event which drew seventeen million people. Cunha popularized hapa-haole music, and his successors included Johnny Noble,** orchestra leader at the Moana Hotel, and Harry Owens, orchestra leader at the Royal Hawaiian, whose 1935 song "Sweet Leilani" became the No. 1 hit nationwide.*** "Sweet Leilani," as sung by Bing Crosby in the movie *Waikiki Wedding*, also won an Oscar for Owens.

Noble openly admired and drew inspiration from the beachboys. *Hula Blues*, a biography about him compiled from his manuscripts, notes, and scrapbooks, states in a chapter on the Moana Pier that "the beachboys and their singing were as much a part of the music of Hawaii as the orchestra within the Moana Hotel, the glee clubs, and the Royal Hawaiian Band." And R. Alex Anderson, whose many compositions included the tune "Sunshine the Beachboy," maintained that the beachboys were among the Islands' best and most sought-after musicians. Their ranks included a number of accomplished entertainers.

Dude Miller. The earliest and perhaps most talented of all the beachboy musicians, Dude Miller played piano and an assortment of stringed instruments, published a popular booklet on the ukulele, and had his own orchestra, the Dude Miller Band. "With the quickness of a tropical rain, he could improvise a melody

A well-known Island painter and composer, beachboy Hiram Anahu wrote a number of popular hits, including "All Because of You," which Al Jolson sang in one of his early movies. Photo courtesy of Steamboat Mokuahi.

---

* The creation of the Hawaiian Homes Commission was intended to rectify injustices done to Hawaiians by setting aside lands that could be leased at a nominal fee by those of at least one-half Hawaiian blood for ninety-nine years.

** Johnny Noble was known as the "Hawaiian Jazz King." A leading figure in hapa-haole music, he wrote such popular hits as "Hula Blues," "My Little Grass Shack," and "Hawaiian War Chant."

*** The popularity of Hawaiian music reached a peak in the 1930s, a lot of it owing to Harry Owens. Blending Hawaiian music with the American ballad, he fashioned a new hapa-haole sound that was in the tradition of Sonny Cunha and Johnny Noble.

A BEACHBOY PARTY/88

on his piano, and by the end of the day would be playing it on at least a half-dozen instruments," wrote Earl Albert Selle in his unpublished biography of Duke Kahanamoku.

Dude was prominent in the heyday of hapa-haole music. In 1915, he was a guest performer at the Panama-Pacific International Exposition. In the same year, he was invited to New York to perform in and direct the show *Stop, Look and Listen*, starring the famous French artist Gaby Deslys. According to *Hula Blues*, Dude and his boys were the talk of New York (his 1935 obituary in the *Honolulu Advertiser* said that he "received nine curtain calls at one performance"). They later toured cities all across the country.

Hiram Anahu. When "famed-beachboy" Hiram Anahu died in 1949, his obituary noted that he had served in various capacities in the household of Queen Liliuokalani and was a well-known Island painter and composer. After graduating from the Kamehameha School for Boys, Anahu turned down a scholarship to study art in Paris and became a beachboy. He ran the business end of the beach concession at the Moana Hotel, taught surfing to visiting dignitaries such as the Duke of Windsor and Lord Mountbatten, and played ukulele on Island radio in a group called the Waikiki Stonewall Boys. Anahu is best remembered, however, as the composer of a number of popular hits, including "All Because of You," which was sung by Al Jolson in one of his earlier movies.

Charlie Amalu. Early beachboy musicians were among Honolulu's best dressed men. Dude Miller established the tradition and was followed by Charlie Amalu, a soft crooner who played ukulele and wore "hand-blocked Panama hats and white Irish-linen suits." Amalu was a direct descendant of royalty, a member of the Lunalilo family, Hawaii's second ruling dynasty. In the 1930s, he was part of a well-known beachboy troupe that included Splash Lyons, Elmer Lee, and Rennie ("Tidal Wave") Brooks. Amalu, who played in Johnny Noble's orchestra when he was at the Royal Hawaiian Hotel, later owned the popular Waikiki nightclub Hawaiian Town. He also appeared frequently on "Hawaii Calls," the Hawaiian-music radio program launched in 1935 from under the banyan tree of the Moana Hotel. The show was eventually carried by over 750 radio stations worldwide.

Pua Kealoha. Best known as the swimmer who won a gold medal in the 1920 Olympics, Pua Kealoha was also a talented musician. A guitarist in Owens's original orchestra at the Royal Hawaiian Hotel, he played for years on the Matson ships that sailed between Hawaii and the mainland. He could both sing and compose, and he had his own troupe, Pua Kealoha and His Hawaiian Trio, which toured the mainland. According to beachboy Harry Robello, he was a great comedian who grew to huge proportions after his Olympic career ended. "Pua weighed over three hundred pounds and danced the hula," Robello recalled. "He'd put on a hula skirt and a brassiere with coconuts inside, and dance right on the beach! When he put his hat out, everybody would throw money in it. Hell, he use to make more than we did working the water."

Beachboy Chick Daniels was renowned for the song "Lei Aloha," which he wrote with Oscar-winning composer Harry Owens. From the collection of Tim Owens. (Opposite page) Beachboys were sought-after entertainers on the Matson liners that sailed between Hawaii and the mainland. Pictured here, from left, is the troupe of Charlie Amalu, Splash Lyons, Rennie Brooks, and Elmer Lee. Photo courtesy of Kulamanu L. R. Lyons.

WAIKIKI BEACH BOY

The songsheet for the tune "Waikiki Beach Boy" featured legendary beachboy canoe steersman John D. Kaupiko on its cover. Courtesy of Jerry Hopkins.

Chick Daniels. The head beachboy at the Royal Hawaiian Hotel, Chick Daniels serenaded guests on the sand by day and performed at night with his troupe, the Royal Hawaiians. He had a long and distinguished career as an entertainer, performing in Hollywood with the Biltmore Trio, in a Hawaiian opera with the Los Angeles Philharmonic, and on Arthur Godfrey's national radio and television broadcasts. Chick was renowned for his pants-dropping hula and for the song, "Lei Aloha," which he wrote with Owens. "Do you know I dreamed that song one night and it stayed right with me," Chick once said. "I kept offering it around, but nobody wanted it. Then one night Harry Owens heard me sing it at a party. So he put English lyrics to it and we published it."

Squeeze Kamana. Almost all beachboys owned a ukulele. The toylike cousin of the guitar, which was portable and easy to play, became as much a symbol of the beachboy as the surfboard. Few played it better than Squeeze Kamana, however, a beachboy with musical training. Sent to St. Louis School at an early age to develop his talent, he learned to play violin. At age fifteen, after the death of his father, he dropped out of school and joined the Navy. Between 1925 and 1928, he entertained on the Matson ships, working for a short spell afterward as a musician in Hollywood. In 1934, he joined Al ("Kealoha") Perry and the Singing Surfriders, the group which in 1937 became the regular orchestra for "Hawaii Calls."

"Hawaii Calls" was a mixture of both hapa-haole and traditional Hawaiian music, and it often showcased Squeeze's talents. A sensational soloist, he could finger chords with his left hand cupped from above as well as from below the neck of the uke. When he played "The World Is Waiting for the Sunrise," his fingers moved almost too fast to follow.

Squeeze also played banjo, guitar, and piano and was an accomplished singer and songwriter. He composed the tune "Lomi Lomi Suntan" ("Big surf, small surf, one and two / First Break, second break, ocean blue"). His most enduring composition, however, was "Pua-maeole" ("Never Fading Flower"), a song written for his daughter. "My dad had a recurring dream," his son, Squeeze, Jr., recalled. "In his dream a young girl was running towards him. And as she got closer she was growing into a woman. This was his vision for my sister, his never-fading flower. He had the music for over ten years before he got the words."

Splash and **Freckles Lyons.** Of the seven sons born to Rosalie Keliinoi, a legislator from Kauai and the first woman elected to public office in Hawaii, Splash and Freckles Lyons were the two "who hung out at the beach." Despite a shared love for music and the water, the brothers were physically dissimilar: Splash was naturally heavy, while Freckles was unusually thin. Of the two, Splash was distinguished as much by his style as by his music. In his later years, he always wore a black yachting cap. He smoked cigarettes with a holder. And he had a canary-yellow MG. Fastened to the back of it was a red trunk in which he kept his musical instruments.

A versatile musician who appeared on Arthur Godfrey's radio and television broadcasts, Splash sang falsetto and played ukulele. He was a master of the steel guitar, an instrument whose exotic and faraway sound became synonymous with Hawaiian music. Along with Charlie Amalu, Elmer Lee, and Rennie Brooks, he went with millionaire Ben Smith in 1934 to perform in New York. Enroute home that same year, he stopped off in Hollywood, where director John Ford invited him aboard his yacht to sail to the South Pacific. While on that cruise, Splash wrote "In the Heart of Paradise," one of his better-known compositions.

Brother Freckles, a guitarist, also traveled extensively. Legend has it that after dropping out of the Kamehameha School for Boys he was playing his music one day on the beach when a man, impressed with his skill, offered to take him around the world. Freckles talked it over with his guitar and went. He was sixteen years old.

His music eventually took him to Hollywood where, during the late 1920s and early 1930s, he worked as an orchestra musician. In 1935, he returned to Hawaii and went to work for the Inter-Island Steamship Company as an accountant. At night he played music on the boats. But in 1942 he decided "bye-bye accounting, hello music and fun" and returned to Hollywood. Three years later, having contracted tuberculosis, he was back in Honolulu. In Leahi Hospital he awoke one morning and read that his old friend from Hollywood, Bob Hope, was in town. With him were the Andrews Sisters and comedian Jerry Colonna. Freckles phoned Hope and asked if he would come and play for the patients. Hope happily obliged.

Freckles had a reputation as a superb back-up musician—"the guy singers and soloists wanted behind them." He played with legendary Hawaiian slack-key guitarist Gabby Pahinui and behind such well-known singers as Pua Alameida and Alfred Apaka (he appeared on an album with the latter). When he and his brother, Splash, recorded albums, they concealed the fact that their respective trios, Freckles Lyons and His Beachboys and Splash Lyons and His Hawaiians, were actually the same group.

The list of prominent beachboy musicians also includes ukulele players Fat Kala and Panama Dave, guitarist Melvin Paoa, who wrote the song "Waikiki Chickadee"; Kalakaua Aylett, a guitarist and singer whose powerful voice carried several hundred yards from the Moana Hotel's Banyan Courtyard to the

Freckles Lyons (left), Splash Lyons (center), and David Kupele. Freckles and Splash both recorded albums, disguising the fact that their respective trios, Freckles Lyons and His Beachboys, and Splash Lyons and His Hawaiians, were actually the same group. Photo courtesy of Kulamanu L. R. Lyons.

beach at the Royal Hawaiian Hotel; and Mystery Cockett, a left-handed bass player who was also a member of the "Hawaii Calls" orchestra.

The beach served as a breeding ground for a great number of Hawaiian entertainers; indeed, the tradition extends through the 1960s and claims such talents as Moe Keale, Zoulou, and even Don Ho. The beach was a great place to learn. And, of course, it was a great place to be discovered. Waikiki was the center of Hawaiian music. Everything happened at the Moana and Royal Hawaiian hotels. Everything was broadcast from "on the beach at Waikiki."

Moreover, at Waikiki a beachboy had a receptive audience. Tourists who came to Waikiki and hung around a beachside bar were easily captured by Hawaiian music. And who better to do it than the beachboys! Their songs embraced the emotional spectrum, and their engaging style had the power to transport one to the very heart of the Hawaiian experience.

No one understood this better than Arthur Godfrey. "Minoaka," or Redhead as he was called, first learned to play the ukulele in the 1920s from a Hawaiian seaman whom he had met in the Navy. One night in 1944, while stranded in Honolulu as an unknown CBS war correspondent, he wandered into The Willows, a popular Honolulu restaurant which after hours became the scene of many great parties. The Willows was managed by Kathleen Perry, wife of musician Al ("Kealoha") Perry, and she remembered Godfrey as "that lonely guy in wrinkled khaki who found The Willows and learned to stay up all night playing Hawaiian songs." Regularly, he returned with his uke to sit in with Squeeze and other members of the Singing Surfriders.

Hawaii altered Godfrey profoundly. Long after he became famous he faithfully promoted Hawaiian music, toting a ukulele wherever he went. In the 1950s when he came out with his Vega-brand baritone ukulele (which bore his name and was marketed nationally), he presented the first one to Squeeze Kamana, and thereafter always sent a Vega uke and a Virginia ham to his beachboy friends at Christmas.

Godfrey's experience was not unusual. What he walked into that night at The Willows—what many people have walked into over the years—was a Hawaiian-style party. Generally speaking, a Hawaiian-style party and a beachboy party are synonymous. Get a group of Hawaiians in a festive mood and pretty soon, usually after a few drinks, they erupt into music. It is all spontaneous, unrehearsed.

A beachboy party is more easily experienced than defined. Some have called it an exercise in making something from nothing; others, a monument to excess. One thing everyone probably would agree on, however, is that a beachboy party is a participatory event. Everybody gets in on the act.

Hawaiian singer Charles K. L. Davis,[*] who for many years worked as an entertainer in Waikiki, recalled how in the evenings the beachboys would gather with a gang of girls and some beer and get them going with songs like "Come on, Nancy, swing around your blouse / Shake those knockers, ring those bells / Come on, Nancy, swing around your blouse."[*] The evenings also gave rise to a number of humorous hulas. The more colorful ones included the "baseball hula" (the pitcher does a slow-motion wind-up, the batter

[*] Opera singer Charles K.L. Davis has performed in Russia, at the Hollywood Bowl, and on network television.

Beachboy musician and prankster Melvin Paoa, pictured here with his guitar, wrote the song "Waikiki Chickadee," which became a favorite at Waikiki. Photo courtesy of Melvin Paoa, Jr.

Crooner Bing Crosby with beachboys (from left) Pua Kealoha, Chick Daniels, and Joe Minor. Photo courtesy of Joanne Makalena Takatsugi.

swings and misses), the "Japanese hula" (the dancer squats like a sumo wrestler, mimicking Japanese guttural sounds and facial contortions); the "cocktail-shake hula" (a great mixer, it is performed with thermos jug in hand), and the "bucking-horse hula" (Chick Daniels, the midnight cowboy, rides again).

Of course, a beachboy party also involved fairly heavy drinking. Legend has it that in the 1930s tourists in Waikiki used to go to the wrestling matches and afterward to the Lau Yee Chai Chinese restaurant to party with the beachboys and watch Sam ("Colgate") Nawai drink. Colgate would start at the top of the liquor list and drink *every* drink on the list. In another version of the beachboy party, Francis Ii Brown, a wealthy and well-known part-Hawaiian sportsman and bon vivant, would rent a suite at the Royal Hawaiian, stock a table with fine liquor, and invite the beachboys up for breakfast, slipping them each a hundred-dollar bill to stay the day and entertain him.*

But a beachboy party was more than just a wild time. Behind the music a philosophy was imparted, a not-so-subtle reminder that singing and laughter were important. The beachboys themselves did not just espouse this philosophy, they lived it. It was part of what made them so irresistible. Consider, for example, the case of Freckles Lyons. Not long after recovering from his bout with tuberculosis, he learned that he had cancer. The doctors told him he had a month to live. What did Freckles do? What would any beachboy do? He got his own private hospital room, stocked a refrigerator with beer, and started singing to the nurses.

Freckles died in 1959, at a time when popular nightclubs such as the Barefoot Bar at Queen's Surf were successfully using the beachboy-party format (an intimate gathering where guests take part in the show) as an entertainment concept. In 1964, the concept became the theme for an album, *A Beachboy Party*, produced by Hawaiian-fashion entrepreneur "Waltah" Clarke.

Like many men of his generation, Clarke was a mainland haole who fell in love with Hawaii and yearned to be a beachboy. After arriving at Waikiki in 1937, he worked at an assortment of odd jobs, including writing a gossip column called "Hawaiian Holidays," which ran in such papers as the *Los Angeles Times* and the *Chicago Tribune* and which he wrote from Waikiki Beach—"third umbrella from the left." In 1952, he opened up a shop that specialized in Hawaiian imports and became successful in the field of

Beachboy Pua Kealoha composed the "Bucking Horse Hula," which was recorded by Chick Daniels and his Royal Hawaiians. (Following page) The Waikiki Stonewall Boys, featuring beachboy Hiram Anahu, were a popular recording group who sang on Island radio. From the DeSoto Brown Collection.

* An accomplished golfer in the 1920s and 1930s, Brown won the Hawaiian, California, and Japan Amateur Championships and set course records at St. Andrews in Scotland and at Pebble Beach in California.

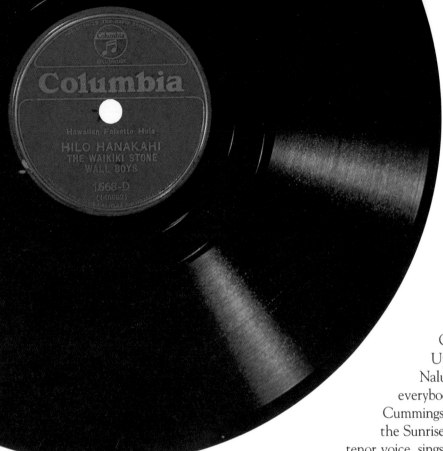

Hawaiian resort wear. Eventually, he opened up twenty-six stores nationwide and built a house in Palm Springs next to houses owned by Frank Sinatra and Spiro Agnew.

It was with money from his clothing empire that Clarke financed *A Beachboy Party*, which is a tribute to the music of the beach. Featured on the album are most of the beachboys who then were still alive—Chick Daniels, Squeeze Kamana, Splash Lyons, Panama Dave, Kalakaua Aylett, and others. In a wonderful cover photograph they are seated with Duke around a torchlit canoe, attired in aloha shirts and holding their guitars and ukes. Bottles of beer serve as props in the foreground.

Clarke, who serves as master of ceremonies on the album, tries to re-create a beachboy party. Appropriately, it begins with Owens' Hawaiian drinking song, "Okole Maluna" ("Bottoms Up"), and ends with the beachboy anthem, "We Love You, Hui Nalu," a song composed for the 1914 "Hui Nalu Follies." In between, everybody gets in on the act. Kalakaua delivers a soulful rendition of Andy Cummings's "Waikiki." Squeeze's ukulele soars on "The World Is Waiting for the Sunrise." Chick croons "Lei Aloha," and Panama, in his best scratchy tenor voice, sings "Cafe Life."

The album has its moments—and its shortcomings. For one thing, the attempt to re-create a beachboy party often seems forced. Still, the beachboy magic that Clarke was trying to capture does come across.

Wherever the beachboys performed—indeed, wherever they went—they took that magic with them. Harry ("Kealoha") Devine, a San Francisco architect whose association with the beach dates back to 1938, tells a story about a day in 1962 when he accompanied Chick Daniels and Turkey Love to the last game of the Giants-Yankees World Series at San Francisco's Candlestick Park. Devine was living in Sacramento at the time, and after the game the three of them drove in his Cadillac convertible to a restaurant called India House.

According to Devine, it was about 1 A.M. when they left the restaurant. Chick and Turkey were carrying a tub of curry that they had ordered to take home, and when they got to Devine's car, he opened the trunk, placed the keys on an inside ledge, put the curry in the trunk, and then slammed the lid, locking the keys inside. When Devine realized what he had done, he was beside himself. They were miles from Sacramento, it was past midnight, and Devine had no spare key. The only other way into the turnk was through a narrow opening behind the back seat, which was too small to accommodate any of them.

(Opposite page) "A Beachboy Party," featured (from left on the sand) Splash Lyons, Fat Kala, and Panama Dave Baptiste; (on canoe) Squeeze Kamana, Ox Keaulani, Jimmy Haku-ole, and Duke Kahana-moku; and (standing) Waltah Clarke, Kala-kaua Aylett, Harry Robello, and Chick Dan-iels. Album courtesy of Ruth Hakuole; reprint-ed with permission from Waltah Clarke.

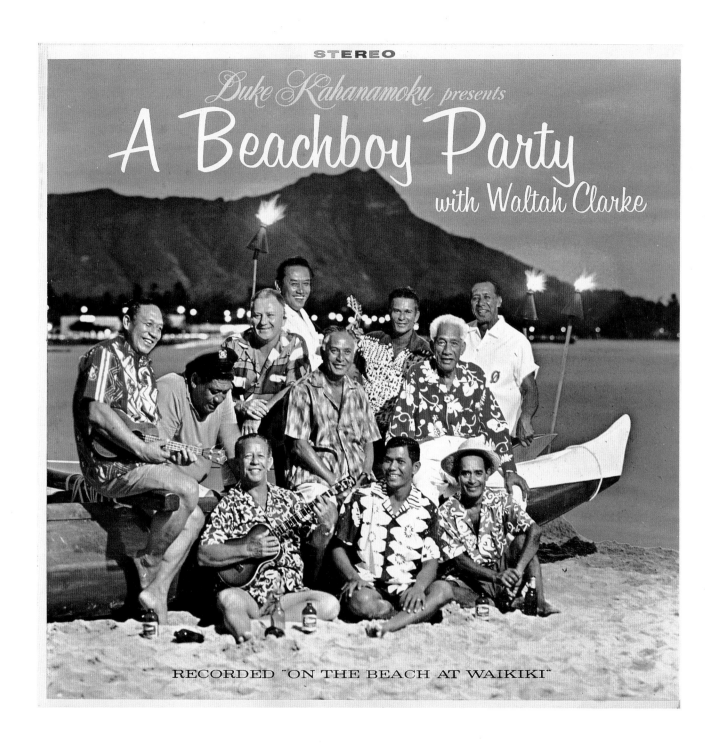

STEREO

Duke Kahanamoku presents

A Beachboy Party

with Waltah Clarke

RECORDED "ON THE BEACH AT WAIKIKI"

"I turned to Chick and Turkey, who were leaning against the car strumming their ukuleles and laughing," Devine recalled, "and I said, 'What we need now is a menehune [a Hawaiian leprechaun]!' And just as I said it, I looked up and swinging down Washington Street was this midget." A pause. "I didn't believe it, either. However, I stopped him and explained our predicament and offered him twenty dollars if he would climb into the trunk and retrieve my keys."

Devine swore that this was a true story, and that not only did the midget climb into the trunk and retrieve the keys, but that afterward, when he turned to give him the twenty dollars, the midget had vanished.

It was a rather disbelieving Harry Devine who climbed in behind the wheel of his Cadillac and drove the ninety miles back to Sacramento that night. It was under clear skies, he recalled, and as they sped down the highway with the top down, Chick and Turkey sat in the back seat strumming their ukes and singing Hawaiian songs. "Have you ever had an experience that stayed with you?" said Devine. "The drive home that night was like that. The music those guys played—I can't describe it. But to this day, I can still hear it. Their voices, the songs. The exact sound of it. It still comes back to me."

Although he did not say as much, Devine had been privy to one of those rare moments when ordinary judgment is suspended and one experiences something extraordinary. Something similar probably happened to Arthur Godfrey at The Willows and to the tourists who once gathered on Sunday evenings on the Moana Pier. The power of the beachboys to "weave a spell of the real Hawaii" over an audience was a singular gift—and the reason they became so popular. Indeed, how else can one explain that when Freckles Lyons went off to that big beach in the sky, both the Mayor of Honolulu and the Governor of Hawaii attended his funeral. In Freckles's honor, a beachboy party was declared for one year. It started that night.

With spirits high, let's drink the cups dry
to the stars above, Okole Maluna
We'll drink to the hula maidens, dancing along the shore
And to you sweetheart, aloha, I love you forever more
Okole Maluna, Okole Maluna
May the ships at sea never be bottoms up,
Okole Maluna

With Hilo Hattie out front, Al "Kealoha" Perry and the Singing Surfriders were the regular orchestra for "Hawaii Calls," the Island radio program once heard on 750 stations worldwide. Members of the "Hawaii Calls" orchestra included leader Al Perry (third from left), and beachboys Mystery Cockett (far left) and Squeeze Kamana (fourth from left). From the Hawaii State Archives.

Rennie "Tidal Wave" Brooks demonstrates how he got his nickname. Photo courtesy of Steamboat Mokuahi.

Steamboat steals the spotlight with a hula at the old Tropics nightclub. Photo courtesy of Steamboat Mokuahi.

Jimmy Durante frolics on the sand fronting the Royal Hawaiian Hotel with beachboys (front to back) Johnny Hollinger, Colgate Nawai, and Tough Bill Keaweamahi. Photo courtesy of Charlie Lambert. Hand-colored by Ron Hudson.

AMBASSADORS OF ALOHA

Friendship, a Handshake and a Bottle of Scotch

5

My fondest [Hawaiian] memories are of the Waikiki beachboys who tried to teach me how to surf, but couldn't. They just paddled me out to where the waves were breaking and held me up on the board. None of them would accept my money for those surfing lessons, but they'd spend their own money on leis, putting so many flowers on me that sometimes I had trouble turning my head. I loved those guys.

—Cary Grant

Cary Grant no doubt regarded the beachboy-tourist relationship as one based on "friendship, a handshake, and a bottle of scotch." Like many others who booked passenger cruises to Waikiki in the years before the Second World War, Grant established a bond of friendship with the beachboys that was genuine and rewarding.

Back then, when Waikiki was a seasonal rite of the rich and famous, beachboys were on the cutting edge of a unique cultural exchange. Legend says that they were a kind of one-man tourist bureau—a combination surfing instructor and social director who provided visitors with the unique Island welcome known as "aloha." However one defines aloha—and it is often defined as "love, freely, spontaneously, and generously given"—the beachboys were said to embody it.

But were they really such innocents? So selfless in their motives? There are those who would argue that they were not—that, in fact, they were highly skilled in the game of separating rich men from their money. This is not in keeping with the legend, but it does point up the hard question: what role did money play at Waikiki? While it is true that the coming of the carriage trade spawned and supported the beachboy profession, this is not the same as saying that money formed the basis of the beachboy-tourist relationship.

Aloha once had real meaning beyond its use as a promotional slogan. A beachboy showed his aloha by taking tourists wherever he went, by including them in everything he did. There was acceptance without deference and a consummate loyalty. For a red-headed East Coast tourist who loved the water but blistered easily in the sun, aloha was going surfing with Molokai Horner. At six o'clock in the morning. In his pajamas. For a California architect, aloha was answering his doorbell in the dead of winter and finding that Fat Kala had come from Hawaii to serenade him with his ukulele. For a former assistant manager at the Royal Hawaiian Hotel, aloha was finding out that the beachboys had lined up to donate blood for an operation he needed—never mind that the blood had to be thrown out because the alcohol content was too high.

Woody Brown, the transplanted Waikiki beachboy who in 1948 helped design and build the modern-day catamaran, is one of many who believe that the 1940s were the "last days" of aloha, that in the aftermath of the Second World War and the accompanying tourist boom, Hawaii's exclusivity and innocence were lost. In 1938, Brown broke the world's distance record in a glider plane with a 263-mile flight from Wichita Falls, Texas, to Wichita, Kansas. In the ensuing days he was deluged with telegrams and paraded through the streets in a Rolls Royce that had its top cut off. That same week his wife died in childbirth.

Shattered, Brown decided he would travel and see the world. He arrived in Hawaii in 1941, and sporting a pair of shorts and a long face, he set out around the island of Oahu on a bicycle. Out near Laie on Oahu's

Actor Cary Grant's admiration of the beach-boys knew no bounds. "I loved those guys," he said. Photo by Joe Akana. (Opposite page) Bing Crosby enjoys the thrills of outrigger canoe surfing in 1936 with Sally Hale, captain of the Waikiki Beach Patrol. From the Hawaii State Archives.

windward coast, a five-year-old Hawaiian boy befriended him and brought him home for dinner. Brown recalled walking into the boy's home, which was sparsely furnished except for a lone upstairs room filled with marvelous Polynesian artifacts—*koa*-wood furniture, *pandanus* and *lauhala* mats, *tapa* cloth, and the like. "It was the most beautiful room in the house," said Brown. "But it was unlived in."

The room was reserved for guests, and the family invited Brown to stay with them. That night, as he was falling asleep, he heard the young boy enter the room. The next thing he knew the boy had climbed into bed and, in an affectionate gesture of hospitality, thrown his arms around him. Said Brown, "Afterward I lay awake thinking to myself, 'My God, what kind of people are these!'"

Those who knew Waikiki in the years before the war say it was like a big family that swelled in size during the winter and summer months. The rich, who brought their fancy cars, came for extended stays with their families. They played hard and spent big, built or bought residences, and in their own way were as eccentric as the beachboys they associated with.

There was Major Douglas King and his wife Ruth, who came by ship from England to the East Coast, by train to the West Coast, and then by ship to Waikiki. The Kings brought their own china and silverware and stayed at the Royal Hawaiian in a double suite with two maids and a pair of dogs. Bill Kahanamoku was their beachboy.

There was Christopher Holmes, heir to the Fleischmann Yeast fortune, who installed electric surfboard gates at his Queen's Surf estate and whose family bought Coconut Island on the windward side of Oahu, stocking it with monkeys, chimpanzees, an elephant, a shark pond, a cannon, and a yacht that came equipped with a bowling alley.* Holmes liked to pal around with Chick Daniels and Pua Kealoha.

There was "dollar-dripping" Doris Duke, the world's wealthiest woman, who built Shangri-la, a $2 million fantasy retreat at Diamond Head that had fountains and waterfalls; chattering ring-tailed and rhesus monkeys; gold, green, and red parrots and parakeets; and "hundreds" of cats. Duke was a friend of the Kahanamoku brothers.

The register at the Royal Hawaiian Hotel in those days read like the cast of a blockbuster Hollywood movie: Douglas Fairbanks and Mary Pickford, Carol Lombard and William Powell, Al Jolson and Ruby Keeler, Shirley Temple, Bing Crosby, Cary Grant, and Charlie Chaplin. Dorothy Mackaill, a star of the silent screen, once explained to a writer why she took up permanent residence at the hotel. "You see more people here, darling, than any other place in the world," she said. "And the best part of it is that, *here,* they are in a festive mood. At home they're different. It's a regular Jekyll and Hyde situation. I don't give people a chance on their home ground. I don't look them up."

The rich found at Waikiki a tonic for their bodies and unrivaled peace of mind. The waters were therapeutic. The trades winds soothing. There was sunshine and serenity. Alfred ("Molokai") Horner, a part-Hawaiian, part-English-Irish beachboy from the island of Molokai, recalled the salubrious effects

*Chris Holmes came to Hawaii in 1926 and later became president of Hawaiian Tuna Packers. His oceanside home at Queen's Surf was across from where the Honolulu Zoo now stands. He also owned Feather Hill Ranch in Santa Barbara, which was the largest private zoo in the United States.

Waikiki had on a wealthy undertaker he once cared for, Bill Hammersmith of San Francisco. Hammersmith came to Waikiki in a wheelchair and in need of exercise. "I used to carry the bugga—lift him off the wheelchair, walk him down, put him in the water," said Molokai. "I'd take him every day. And every day he'd give me a dime. I don't know what made me save those dimes, but I saved them. I used to get ice water for him, things like that. Everytime I do something for him—dime.

"The day before he left, he called me. 'Hey, Molokai, you still got all those dimes I was giving you?' 'Yeah.' I thought the cheap bastard wanted them back. But ho, ho, ho—for every dime, he gave me a five-dollar bill. I made a couple hundred bucks! Afterward he said, 'You know, Molokai, when I was young, all I wanted to do was make a million dollars. When I made my first million, all I wanted was to make ten million. I got awful greedy. Look at me now. But Waikiki has helped.'" And it was true. Although Bill Hammersmith came to Waikiki in a wheelchair, he left walking with a cane.

B eachboy-tourist relationships could develop in a number of ways. Sometimes the relationship resulted from a referral, sometimes from a surfing lesson. Sometimes tourists were assigned a beachboy. There was not much a beachboy did not do. He was water instructor, entertainer, tour guide, chauffeur, and baby-sitter. To some extent he was a retainer; it was his job to be in attendance, to be available. But he was not a "yes" man and he did not poach.

George ("Airedale") McPherson, who spent his summers as a beachboy prior to the war, defined the beachboy's true status as a companion or guardian. The attitude among the beachboys, he said, was that "nobody touches these people. They are in our protective custody, they are our guests."

The role that money played in the relationship is difficult to assess. The popular assumption is that money was not important to the beachboys, that it had no important place in their value system. However, there is evidence that suggests otherwise. Panama Dave, for instance, used to refer to his rich friends as "sponsors." And on boat days (which were also known as pay days), Chick Daniels used to arm himself with leis and reap huge rewards. Chick had different kinds of leis for different categories of tippers. For example, a crown-flower or a milkweed lei was reserved for a fifty-dollar tipper. A plumeria lei for a hundred- to two-hundred dollar tipper. A carnation lei for a five-hundred dollar tipper. "When you saw

Is the humor in this postcard intended or an accident? Passenger ships coming to Hawaii have always docked at Honolulu Harbor, not Waikiki Beach. From the Baker-Van Dyke Collection.

that pikake," a fellow beachboy recalled, "that's a gold mine. At least a thousand dollars."

Even taking care of children was, for some, done with an eye on profit. Many beachboys preferred the company of children to adults because, as one beachboy put it, "if you treat them good, they drain the parents." The beachboys all knew who spent money and who did not. Turkey Love recalled that Art Linkletter, who came to Waikiki after the war, did not. "That guy, everytime I'm out teaching someone to surf, he'd hang around and say, 'Is this wave okay to catch? Is this the way to do it?' He'd never take a lesson. Too cheap. That was Art Linkletter. He made like a bird."

It is also true that a high percentage of beachboy stories, even the most touching ones, involve money. And, of course, beachboys love to talk about the big tips they made. Airedale McPherson recalled with particular clarity a rich Jewish family that came to Waikiki one winter. They had a young boy named Eric, who was six, possibly seven, and it was Airedale's job to teach him how to swim. He took him out in the baby surf in front of the Royal Hawaiian and taught him how to hold his breath underwater. All was fine until the boy suddenly became restless.

"Airedale, this is no fun," he said. "Take me out and let's go catch a wave!"

"Eric, you can't even swim, you little meathead! If you fall off that board, you'll drown."

"Yes, but you won't let me fall off—so let's go!"

Airedale got out his old redwood plank—"which must have weighed 170 pounds; I mean, if you could carry it, steal it"—and together he and the boy caught two waves. When they came in, Airedale threw his board on the sand and was heading up the beach when who should he see standing at the corner of the Royal Hawaiian but young Eric's father, who summoned him with an imperious wave of his forefinger. Airedale, who was only a teenager, figured he had had it. By taking the boy out surfing before he could swim he had broken a cardinal rule.

"Yessir?" Airedale said.

"Young man, I want to thank you," the father announced.

"Sir?"

"I want to thank you for giving my son the best day he's had in his life so far."

And with that the father held out his hand, and when Airedale shook it he felt something. When the man left, he opened his hand and to his astonishment discovered a hundred dollar bill!

Obviously, the beachboys were aware of money. But it would be an overstatement to say that they were preoccupied with money. They certainly were not preoccupied with accumulating it. Big tips were spent as fast as they were made. Jerry Hallinan, a title-insurance executive from San Francisco and a long-time visitor to Waikiki, recalled that with the exception of Chick Daniels most of the beachboys did

Actor Douglas Fairbanks received a warm welcome, including a lei from Duke Kahanamoku, when he arrived at the Royal Hawaiian Hotel in 1927. From the Hawaii State Archives. (Opposite page) The legendary Will Rogers made his one and only trip to Hawaii in 1934. Here he is serenaded by the beachboy troupe of (from left) Charlie Amalu, Splash Lyons, Elmer Lee, and Rennie Brooks. Photo courtesy of Kulamanu L. R. Lyons.

not make much money. And what money they did make, they shared among themselves. "One thing about those boys, they were always together," he said. "And if one guy had money and the other one didn't, it didn't make any difference. He'd just give it to the other guy. That was the aloha spirit. I tell you, those boys were just like something out of a book."

Hallinan came to Waikiki in 1926 and was assigned to George ("Tough Bill") Keaweamahi.* Tough Bill was a kind of gentle giant. He stood six feet four, and his nickname was derived from his brute strength. Legend has it that he could bend a fifty-cent piece with his fingers and pop the cap off a bottle of beer with his thumb. Hallinan knew Tough Bill when, as a side job, he was driving a police patrol in Waikiki. At the time, Hallinan stayed at the Halekulani Hotel, and every morning his wife went for a Swedish massage across town. "At seven o'clock every morning Tough Bill would swing by in his buggy, pick up my wife, and take her for her massage," Hallinan recalled. "Those days are gone."

A fierce loyalty, not money, cemented the beachboy-tourist relationship, and that loyalty worked in both directions. "A very peculiar thing," said Hallinan. "You didn't dare insult those boys. I remember the one time Tough Bill asked me for money. He approached me right on the beach and said, 'Jerry, give me twenty dollars.' He'd been drinking and looked like hell, and I didn't want to give him the money because I knew he'd just use it to buy more booze. However, I gave it to him. He was gone for about ten or fifteen minutes and then he came back. And he handed me the twenty dollars. I said, 'Keep it, Tough Bill. Why the hell did you ask me for twenty dollars if you want to give it back?' He said, 'Jerry, I just wanted to see if you were my friend.' Imagine that! But they were all that way. If you were their friend, you were their friend."

Did Hallinan sense in that episode a peculiar logic? Did he feel manipulated? "Hell no," he maintained. "I knew what he meant." Such loyalty was actually reassuring to the rich; truly trustworthy companions were hard to find. But the beachboys also tempered their loyalty with humor—and often at the tourists' expense. For tourists it was good therapy. In fact, comedy as a form of therapy was one of the main remedies available at Waikiki.

Tough Bill, for instance, was one of many beachside comedians. A 1930 tourist booklet, *Highlights on Honolulu,* noted that he worked as a "beach comforter" at the Royal Hawaiian Hotel, circulating "sunshades, coconut oil, amusement, and whatnot among the guests." He also did a terrific hula and was the animated conductor of a beachboy orchestra, a motley crew that tucked their ukuleles under their chins and played them like violins.

Usually Tough Bill worked with Bill ("Tarball") Kahanamoku, who was short and hunchbacked. Together they entertained tourists with impersonations and other routines. Tough Bill would stand at the water's edge and make a circle with his arms; Tarball would run and try to dive through it. There is a story about a famous muscleman who once came to Waikiki and shamelessly strutted along the beach in brief, revealing swim wear. One day Tough Bill and Tarball stuffed wads of seaweed down the front of their

*Tough Bill Keaweamahi was pure Hawaiian and played Chief Milu in the movie *Aloha Hawaii.* He also was a member of a well-known beachboy family. His brothers, Steamboat Bill and Major Dan, were founding members of Hui Nalu.

Duke and Duke. In his last film role in 1948, Duke Kahanamoku played alongside John "Duke" Wayne in *Wake of the Red Witch.* Photo courtesy of Kimo Wilder McVay. (Opposite page) During the filming of *Bird of Paradise* in 1931, beachboy Chick Daniels entertains stars Joel McCrea and Dolores Del Rio. Others in the photo are the make-up man and hairdresser. Photo courtesy of Joanne Makalena Takatsugi.

Beachboy Joe Akana (at right) with the Maharajah of Indore, his wife, and Johnny Gomez. The Maharajah, who came to Waikiki in 1936, was one of the world's richest men. He later took Akana on a trip down the West Coast. Photo courtesy of Joe Akana.

bathing suits and fell into step behind him. That was surfside comedy at its best, and the tourists howled.

"The beachboys were very colorful, very amusing," recalled Chris Cusack, the president of a Honolulu insurance firm and a veteran member of the Outrigger Canoe Club. "They didn't cater to rich. And they seldom got out of hand. They were smart enough not to. However, they all knew what the bottom line was, and that was getting the tourists to pay."

Cusack was ten years old when he came to Waikiki in 1927. His stepfather, a dockside reporter, had been friends with writer Jack London and was a great admirer of the beachboys. It was an admiration Cusack came to share. "There was a definite 'in' feeling the tourists got with the beachboys," he recalled. "They weren't on the outside looking in. I suppose it was like going to Spain and meeting the matadors. Many of the rich had no intention of meeting the important local people here. Doris Duke was a great example of that. She could have socialized with the Cookes and the Dillinghams, but she had no interest in it. She liked the beachboys. They amused her."

Tobacco heiress Doris Duke was the tall, golden-haired daughter of James B. Duke, president of the American Tobacco Company. In 1935, she came to Hawaii with her first husband, James Cromwell, a New York economist who was recently divorced from Delphine Dodge of the Detroit auto family. Duke was a reluctant socialite who disdained the press and used Hawaii as a hideaway. She knew all the Kahanamokus, especially Sam, who became her caretaker at Shangri-la. In 1939, she and Sam won first prize in a tandem surfboard-paddling race at Waikiki.

Beachboy Melvin Paoa, a first cousin of the Kahanamokus who took care of James Cromwell's daughter, Christine, was also close to Doris Duke. Paoa was a notorious beachboy prankster who later became a fireman. Among other things, he was known for slipping Mickey Finns into drinks and shaving off the eyebrows of fellow beachboys when they passed out at parties. There is a story that while answering a call he once drove his fire truck out of a Honolulu station, rounded a corner, and ran head-on into the front window of a department store. It was characters like Paoa who kept Duke amused.

Paoa recalled a trip he took in the late 1930s with his best friend and fellow beachboy Dutchy Wilhelm, in which they visited Duke at her estate in Sommerville, New Jersey. The two beachboys, who had left Los Angeles with only a can of salmon and a bag of poi, hitchhiked across country and arrived in New York with seven dollars between them. "We were staying on Third and Fifty-first," said Paoa. "There was a train upstairs and every time it went by it rattled the garbage cans outside our door." Paoa decided to call Doris Duke.

"What are you guys doing here?" she asked.

"Vacation," he told her.

"You guys are always on vacation. Why don't you come see me. I'll have someone pick you up tomorrow."

The next morning a chauffeured limousine picked them up at Third and Fifty-first and took them to Duke's estate. "Wow, what a place!" said Paoa. "Two-thousand-something acres. Her own police force. Her own cop on a motorcycle!" For two weeks the beachboys lived like kings. Every night there were guests for dinner, and Duke flew with them to Washington, D.C. When it was time to return to Honolulu, Duke booked them on the *Lurline*. According to Paoa, they came back first class.

As a measure of their friendship, the rich frequently took the beachboys with them on trips. In fact, many beachboys seemed to have spent as much time on boats and planes as they did on the beach. An obituary noting the death of Tough Bill Keaweamahi in 1955 revealed that he had been around the world *seven* times.

Panama Dave Baptiste and a young Mickey Rooney have their own beachside party. Photo courtesy of Charlie Lambert.

There were, of course, other benefits. William Clarke, a Montana copper magnate, paid for Pua Kealoha's education at St. Louis School. He also paid for Sam Kahanamoku's education at the Honolulu Military Academy. Doris Duke gave Sam a house near Diamond Head that had once served as living quarters for her gardener, and Splash Lyons, beachboy for playboy-millionaire George Vanderbilt, got the down payment for his house from the scion's family.*

Waikiki was a place of great opportunity for a beachboy—and that opportunity extended to the motion-picture industry. Prior to the Second World War, beachboys were used as extras in such films as *Bird of Paradise*, starring Joel McCrea and Dolores Del Rio, and *Waikiki Wedding*, starring Bing Crosby, Anthony Quinn, and Martha Raye. After the war, beachboys appeared in *Hard Bargain*, *Big Jim McLain*, *Rampage*, *Mr. Roberts*, and *The Old Man and the Sea*.

Harry Robello, who left the beach during the 1950s to work in Hollywood, was one of several beachboys who were members of the Screen Actors Guild. A handsome, quick-witted Portuguese who spoke colorful pidgin English, Robello is always referred to as the "smart" beachboy, the one who was able to capitalize on his associations with Waikiki. He was a crack golfer (a three handicap), and partly due to a golfing friendship with Richard Holtzman, general manager of Sheraton Hotels in Hawaii, he later took over the

*George Vanderbilt inherited $40 million and maintained a home in Honolulu for twenty-one years. He was a descendant of railroad tycoon Cornelius Vanderbilt, who built one of the largest family fortunes in America.

Beachboy • Harry Ro-
bello (in uniform) on set
in Hollywood with Gene
"Hukilau" Bryant, a
unit production manag-
er for 20th Century-
Fox. Robello and Bryant
had a friendship that
spanned some thirty
years. Photo courtesy of
Harry Robello.

lucrative Sheraton beach concession in Waikiki. He became a member of two of Honolulu's most prestigious clubs: the Outrigger Canoe Club and the Oahu Country Club. He also built up a stock portfolio that, according to friends, "would choke a horse."

Robello was the beachboy for Cybil and Harry Brandt, the director for publicity at 20th Century-Fox, and it was indirectly through Brandt that he got his start in the movie industry. Later, he became the companion and confidant of Gene ("Hukilau") Bryant, a production manager for 20th Century-Fox. Bryant, who was something of a beachboy in spirit, headed straight for Waikiki between pictures. He and Robello enjoyed a friendship that spanned some thirty years. "Gene wasn't much of a waterman," Robello recalled. "In fact, he neva even went in the water. But as for good times—yeah. He was just like Chick and Panama. He was like a beachboy."

When Bryant came to Waikiki, he sometimes chartered a plane and took the beachboys to the Neighbor Islands. When it was time to return to Hollywood, the beachboys would accompany him to the airport, start drinking, and inevitably end up on the plane. At Bryant's home in Beverly Hills, the party would often continue for another couple of days.

Acting became Robello's full-time career when he went to visit Bryant one year at Christmas. One thing led to another and it was eight years before he came back.

In Hollywood, Robello worked mostly as an extra, a role he assumed with good humor. Friends recalled that a director who was impressed with his good looks once cast him in a speaking role as a Navy lieutenant. And then the director heard him talk. But Robello did land some interesting assignments. He handled the "bloodless actors"—that is, the sharks—during the shooting of *12-Mile Reef* and *20,000 Leagues Under the Sea.*

Robello once told a reporter about venturing into a holding tank containing twenty sharks in the Bahamas. "We were picking out the guys for the day's shooting," he explained. "The ones you don't want, you just tap on the nose, they swim away. You net your shark and throw him outside. Put him in a half-sunk rowboat and row him out to work. Then we throw him out, tie a rope on his tail so he can't run away. Then when the director's ready I go down with an aqualung, untie the rope, ride him over to the cameras, and give him a push in the right direction." He paused. "Honest."

Although Robello returned to the beach in 1958, his friendship with Bryant continued. In the mid-1960s Bryant retired from 20th Century-Fox. Then in his sixties and a bachelor all his life, he moved to the Islands, where he lived for almost a decade before returning to California.

A few years later he fell ill. Robello, who had been like a son to Bryant, made repeated trips to help care for him and manage his affairs. When Bryant died, Robello was surprised to learn that Bryant had left him everything, including his house. Robello also inherited a 1960 Cadillac Coup de Ville, which he still keeps in his driveway.

Beachboy Molokai Horner (pictured here) saved the life of millionaire Herb Fox in 1937 and the two became lifelong friends. When Fox died in 1962, Horner gave him a beachboy funeral, scattering his ashes beyond the reef at Waikiki. Photo coutesy of Harry Robello.

Robello's relationship with Bryant is testimony to the strong bond of friendship that existed between many tourists and beachboys. Those who suspect that Robello's goodwill was motivated by what he stood to gain should remember that by the time Bryant died it was Robello, the beachboy, who was the wealthier of the two.

Most beachboys were not in the beachboy business for the money but for the lifestyle it offered—a lifestyle that was widely envied. Indeed, more rich men wanted to be beachboys than beachboys wanted to be rich. To be sure, money was a factor in the beachboys' association with the rich, and no doubt there were some who cultivated a relationship because they stood to profit from it. But beachboy-tourist relationships were not based on money. More often than not, they were based on a deep and abiding friendship.

Perhaps the most famous story about a beachboy and a millionaire is the one about Molokai Horner and Herb Fox, a California racing-car driver and mechanical engineer who later inherited a fortune. Molokai, who was left a small monthly pension when Fox died in 1962, recalled that he met Fox in the 1930s, before he came into his inheritance. The two used to surf and drink together. One day in 1937 Fox was out surfing and his board struck him on the back of his head, knocking him unconscious. Molokai was paddling out and spotted him. He pulled Fox out of the water, put him on his surfboard, and paddled in. "If I didn't get him," said Molokai, "he'd be dead."

Fox never forgot. He took Molokai to the mainland and showed him California. When he got married, he invited Molokai to the reception. Molokai also had the use of the house in back of any residence owned by Fox. In the mid-1950s when Fox learned that Molokai's diabetic mother was going blind, he stepped in and paid for the operation. As a result, Molokai's mother was able to retain sight in one eye.

In 1959, Molokai was able to return the favor. He was back living on Molokai at the time, and that year during the annual Molokai-to-Oahu canoe race, fellow beachboy Steamboat Mokuahi came to deliver a message: Fox had cancer. When Molokai went to Honolulu, he saw that one of Fox's arms had been amputated. When Fox asked him if he would stay with him, Molokai told him, "Anything for you, Herb." "We went up to the mainland and picked up a Rolls Royce," he recalled. "I used to drive him around, things like that. I stayed over a year. Then they found a spot on his lung. When that spot came on, that's it."

Fox was told he had six months to live. Six months to the day, he died. Molokai was with him. "We had a few drinks," he recalled. "Suddenly I could tell he was dead already. No pink, nothing. Just that greyish look. The glass fell out of his hand. I picked the bugga up, took him upstairs, put my hand over his eyes. Later on his wife came in. When she saw him she screamed. I stayed with her about a month. Then I took the ashes out. Waikiki. That's where he wanted. Just like a beachboy."

An outrigger canoe loaded with tourists takes off on a wave at Waikiki in 1938. The woman on the surfboard in the foreground is thought to be Doris Duke. Photo by Ray Jerome Baker, from the Baker-Van Dyke Collection.

Panama Dave, clown prince of the beachboys, always wore a coconut hat. Photo by Scoops Tsuzuki; hand-colored by Ron Hudson.

PANAMA DAVE
The Clown Prince of Waikiki

6

Waikiki is really beautiful. But if you took away the water what would you have? Panama, one of the beachboys, is trying to sell me shares of his seaweed ranch. Do you think it's legitimate?

—Red Skelton

Panama Dave took his name from the canal-wide gap between his two front teeth.* He wore, James Michener once wrote of a fictional counterpart, "his own kind of costume: enormous baggy shorts of silk and cotton that looked like underwear and fell two inches below his knees, a tentlike aloha shirt whose ends he tied about his middle, leaving a four-inch expanse of belly, Japanese slippers with thongs between his toes, and a coconut hat with a narrow brim and two long fibers reaching eight inches in the air and flopping over on one side." He never had a nine-to-five job. He never owned his own house, bought a new car, or made an investment. For more than forty years his business address was Waikiki Beach, his office the nearest bar.

Panama Dave led a comic-book existence. He did not own much. He did not work much. He did not spend much. There was no need for him to do so. He was Waikiki's clown prince, a lovable five feet seven crackerjack who learned early on that his job in life was to keep people laughing.

"This beach life is the only life," he once told a female reporter. "Women to take care of you, penthouse apartments, Cadillac convertibles, hundred-dollar bills under the pillow every morning. It's great and you're still a bachelor."

It was great, except that, as the reporter soon learned, Panama was no longer single.

"So how's married life?" she asked him.

"No different," said Panama.

Panama Dave was one of Waikiki's greatest characters. He was an actor on a different kind of stage, a celebrity in a swimsuit who became almost as famous as those he amused. The rich adored him and showered him with presents. It has been said that a number of women proposed marriage. Children followed him around as if he were the Pied Piper of Hamelin. "Everywhere he went, everything was free," recalled his old friend and fellow beachboy, Turkey Love. "He'd go to the bar and everyone would buy him drinks. And he wouldn't ask. They'd just buy."

While some beachboys were known as watermen and others as musicians, Panama was a personality. His function on the beach was primarily social. His role was to do and say the unexpected thing, to be the life of the party, to be Panama. "He was tirelessly entertaining," recalled one of his benefactors, Jerry Hallinan, a title-insurance executive from San Francisco. "The big wheels who came to Waikiki all sat and laughed with him. Everyone who came to the beach in those days, they all knew Panama."

That is the familiar refrain: *everyone knew Panama.* And yet, for all the attention and notoriety he received, the places he went, the lives he touched, there may never have been a beachboy whom the public seemed to know so well but actually did not.

Panama Dave with Detroit Tiger baseball star Hank Greenberg. Photo courtesy of Charlie Lambert. (Opposite page) The fish may have been big at Waikiki in the old days, but they were not this big. Beachboys (from left) Joe Akana, Melvin Paoa, and Panama Dave Baptiste actually caught this marlin off Oahu's Kaena Point and brought it back to Waikiki. Photo courtesy of Joe Akana.

*No one, not even Panama's brother, John Baptiste, could recall the origin of "Dave" in Panama Dave.

His real name was Charles Kalei Baptiste, Jr. The younger of two sons of a Portuguese-Hawaiian father and a pure Hawaiian mother, he was born in Kualoa, Oahu, in 1909 and raised a few blocks *mauka,* or on the mountain side, of downtown Honolulu. From the beginning, he was what the Hawaiians called a *manuela* boy, a happy-go-lucky boy. As a youth, he was dark and muscular with wavy brown hair. He looked Hawaiian. But, curiously, as he grew older, his Portuguese features became more pronounced. The Portuguese side of him also manifested itself in his humor. Like his father, an elevator man at the Alexander Young Hotel, he was an irrepressible, quick-witted rascal.

In his teens he was a springboard diving champion at the local YMCA, and he often joined the "wharf rats" who dived for coins down at the waterfront. He began working the beach even before he graduated from St. Louis School, entertaining tourists with his stunts on a surfboard.

He acquired his reputation as a clown early on. Panama was naturally funny; everything about him seemed slightly off key. He had a squeaky tenor voice that could always be located in a crowd, and he spoke his own brand of English, mixing metaphors and otherwise mangling the language. At a beachside bar he would gaze seaward and say, "Look, out there on the horizontal," meaning the horizon. He would sum up a problem by noting, "Well, that's the whole kettle of fish in a nutshell." Or he would remind a student of a five o'clock surfing lesson by spelling it out, "That's V-I-V-E."

He was just as bad with names. He boasted that he knew the "Kraft-cheese girls" and "that pistol family—the Colts." "I know those Hormels, too," he once told a writer. "The meat family. One of them married Leslie Caron, and I taught her to surf. She fabulous. She can stand on the board with one feet, just like dancing the burlesque."

The Panama of the beach was a chirpy little comedian who could tweak people's noses one minute and leave them laughing the next. He and Tough Bill had a skit they often performed in the evenings when the tourists were gathering for cocktails. Panama would be out in the water, rolling around in the shallows, and Tough Bill would appear with a canoe paddle. Holding the fat end of the paddle in his hands as if it were a fishing pole, he would start casting. Pretty soon he would have Panama hooked.

A tremendous fight ensued. Tough Bill was the angler trying to land a big one, Panama his fish at the end of the line. And then the line would go limp. The fish was dead, floating toward the bottom. Throwing down his paddle, Tough Bill would run into the water and grab Panama by his shoulders, drag him to shore, drop him on his stomach, and begin pounding on his back. Panama would not come to. Finally, Tough Bill would turn Panama over, lift up his right leg, and bite down on his big toe. "Ouch!" Panama would squeal, releasing a spout of water that arched through the air and struck Tough Bill smack in the face. This triggered uproarious laughter from the tourists. Panama then got up and jumped back in the ocean.

If ever a man found his niche, it was Panama. No other job except being a beachboy would have suited him quite so well. He lived without pretense (and without shoes), teaching surfing in the morning, playing gin rummy in the afternoon, and partying at night while the waves washed the beach clean.

Sooner or later most beachboys got off the beach, but Panama made it his life. By any standard, it is not an easy life to gauge. There are none of the usual indicators one uses to chronicle a man's development.

No important promotions. Few if any career changes. For a beachboy like Panama, the challenges were infrequent, his days marked by a certain comfortable sameness.

The occasions when he left the beach are among the events that help to define Panama's life. In 1930, at age twenty, he joined his cousin Lani McIntire, a popular Island orchestra leader. For two years he performed with his ukulele on West Coast radio stations KMTR and KNX. During the war, he was a driver for the Army stationed at Punahou School. And in 1948, he and Turkey Love worked as extras in a film called *Thieves' Market*. Gene Bryant of 20th Century-Fox got them the job, putting them up for a month at the Palace Hotel in San Francisco. Panama subsequently appeared in at least two other films—*Hard Bargain*, with Richard Conte, and *Big Jim McLain*, starring John Wayne.

Photographs also provide information about Panama and confirm his celebrity status at Waikiki. There he is on the beach playing music with a young Mickey Rooney…here he is sitting with Detroit outfielder Hank Greenberg …there he is having cocktails with John Wayne…now he is having dinner with Rosalind Russell…look at him posing as Gloria Vanderbilt's canoe captain in *Look* magazine.

Photographs tell us that Panama liked to drink. One is particularly revealing. He is seated at a banquet with director John Ford and actress Anna May Wong. He looks somewhat dazed, and a note scribbled next to him explains why. "Had about sixteen highballs when this picture was taken," it reads.

One could usually find Panama at his favorite hangout, the Moana Hotel's Kamaaina Bar. If someone said, "Hey Panama, you wanna drink?" he would always accept. But Panama's drinking sometimes got him in trouble. Beachboys Harry Robello and Turkey Love recalled a Beverly Hills party they once attended with Panama. Afterward, the three of them agreed to meet with their dates at a popular nightspot called the Tail of the Cock. Robello and Turkey went in one car and arrived first. They waited and waited—but no Panama. Finally, his girlfriend showed up alone and told them that Panama was in jail. He had been arrested for drunk driving.

Robello and Turkey found him at a Hollywood police station, spotting his ukulele behind the counter as they walked in.

"We came for Panama," they told the officer on night duty.

"You mean Charles Baptiste?" the officer replied.

"Yeah, that's him."

The officer brought Panama out.

"Bail will be $250."

At a banquet with director John Ford and actress Anna May Wong, Panama Dave looks somewhat dazed. A note scribbled next to him explains why: "Had about sixteen highballs when this photo was taken." Photo courtesy of Charlie Lambert.

Robello and Turkey did not even have to check their wallets.

"Take him back," they said.

As they were leaving, Robello turned to the police officer, "How about giving us his ukulele?"

The officer shook his head. "Sorry, but he's going to entertain *us*."

Panama's special gift was his sense of humor. His life seems a series of anecdotes, each more outrageous than the previous one. But as funny as he was, as charming and affable and upbeat as he was, it could not be said that he was generous. To the contrary, family and friends describe him as a notorious tightwad—the kind of guy who would borrow a dime because he was reluctant to break a quarter or who would excuse himself to make a phone call when it came time to pay the check.

To be fair, he never had much money. And he was generous in other ways. His apartment was home to any number of beachboys, and he was always willing to share the extra business that came his way on the beach. Still, Panama's idea of hospitality—and his favorite expression—was "You can be my host." Or, conversely, "Let me be your guest."

It was Panama who coined the term "sponsors" to describe his rich friends, of which there were many. Alfred S. Bloomingdale, the department-store millionaire who founded Diners Club, was particularly partial to Panama. According to Harry Robello, Bloomingdale was one of the biggest tippers ever to step foot on Waikiki Beach. When he was leaving, he would start down the beach with thousands of dollars in his shirt pocket and ask Panama, "What shall I give this guy?" And Panama would say, "I don't care what you give him. But you give me five-hundred bucks!" And he got it. Once he even got the car Bloomingdale had been driving.

Jerry Hallinan recalled a story about a Texas millionaire, an oil man, who came to Waikiki and made arrangements for Panama to sign checks for him. The millionaire stayed for three weeks, and all the while Panama was picking up tabs and treating everyone. One afternoon he came into the Moana's Kamaaina Bar. He had spent the day taking the millionaire around, and the millionaire had given him a gift—a money clip in the shape of an oil derrick with a diamond on top. Panama was very proud; he passed the money clip around for everyone to admire. When it came to Hallinan, he looked at it and threw it across the table. "What the hell good is this?" he asked. "How can a man give you a money clip and not put any green in it?" Panama sat in silence for a few minutes and then disappeared. A short while later he returned with the money clip. This time the millionaire had filled it with a wad of green.

Not everyone condoned this kind of behavior. For all the camaraderie that existed on the beach, certain tensions existed. In Panama's case some saw past the clown, viewing him as a freeloader. Airedale McPherson recalled that the more conscientious beachboys regarded Panama as a playboy, a guy who amused himself at the expense of others. "Oh, he gave amusement," he said. "He was a great joker. Always a witticism on his lips. But nobody took him seriously. Nobody knew much about him—where he came from or who his father was. He didn't want anybody knowing him as anything but wisecracking, heavy-drinking Panama Dave. Beyond that you could not go."

Lani McIntire and his Island orchestra. In 1930, a twenty-year-old Panama Dave (not pictured here) toured the West Coast, playing his ukulele with this group. Photo courtesy of Charlie Lambert.

*To Panama
Always your Pal
Lani McIntire*

It was Airedale's opinion that Panama's humor was largely defensive, and that beneath the cheerful exterior he was not as happy as he appeared. He said he had a memory of Panama dressed in a suit and wearing shoes. Luckily, they woke him up. Panama had passed out, and the high tide was coming up the beach; it was up to his hips when they got him. Airedale added that different beachboys were on the beach for different reasons. "What Panama wanted out of that beach was anonymity," he said. "And he got it."

Extroverted personalities are sometimes the most enigmatic. Panama's life on the beach *was* largely anonymous. He was Panama Dave, not Charles Baptiste, a cartoonlike character who had a celebrity's access to everything without any of the accompanying responsibilities.

Panama used to deflect questions about his background by giving funny, partially true accounts of himself. In a well-remembered 1956 interview that appeared in the *Honolulu Star-Bulletin*, he told columnist Cobey Black about his past. "I've been on the beach nearly all my life," he said. "Thirty years easy. My family's from down in the country. My mother's pure Hawaiian, and my father's French-Portuguese-Canadian. He came over on a schooner and married my mother."

"Was she beautiful?" Black asked.

"Still is. He is, too."

Panama told Black that he came to the city to go to Central Grammar School. He said it used to be a palace that belonged to one of the Hawaiian princesses, but he did not know which princess. He said his grandfather was in charge of the old sugar mill—"you know, the historic one that's all fallen down, the one made of coral. My mother comes from royalty and has land over there given her by the king."

"Which king?" asked the columnist.

"Kamehameha. I don't know which Kamehameha. She was a friend of Prince Kuhio. I know him, too. A great guy, fat and with a mustache…." Panama told Black about the time he was arrested for drunk driving in California. "My picture was on the front page and the headlines read, 'Famous beachboy swims not only in the Pacific, but in alcohol.'" (Panama's arrest did make front-page news.) He told Black about how he had once been mistaken for "a barefooted millionaire" in San Francisco while he was with trucking magnate Charles Tilden. And how when he went to Texas nobody could figure out if he was Mexican or Indian.

"Have you been to the mainland often?" Black asked.

"Oodles of times," said Panama. "I went to college at Dayton College, Ohio."

"What did you major in?"

"Everything."

Panama never went to college, of course; few beachboys did. His brother claimed his father was not part-Canadian or part-French. Their mother was not descended from royalty. As Panama Dave, however, Charles Baptiste could say these things and get away with them.

Panama's fondness for concealing his identity is best illustrated by the masquerade he pulled off with millionaire Henry J. Topping. The Topping family had made their money in tin. Henry's brother, Dan, owned the New York Yankees and Henry, who was better known as Bob, made a career out of marrying

Millionaire Bob Topping (above). In the late 1930s he and Panama Dave teamed up to pull a huge joke on Honolulu's high society. From the Hawaii State Archives. (Opposite page) On the grounds of the Royal Hawaiian Hotel, a car dealer has Panama Dave behind the wheel for an ad promoting a new 1950s Buick. Looking on are beachboys Steamboat Mokuahi and Curly Cornwell. Photo courtesy of Steamboat Mokuahi.

actresses Arline Judge, Jane Durant, and Lana Turner. In the late 1930s, he and Panama teamed up to play a huge joke on Honolulu's high society. Another front-page newspaper story, this one carrying the headline "Quiet Visit of Maharajah Sets Local Hearts A Flutter" eloquently chronicled their caper.

Without fanfare or other ostentation....without a word of warning or so much as a line in the newspaper, the Maharajah Haider Panjor of India arrived in Honolulu and was spirited away to the home of his host, Henry J. Topping, who is by the way something of a celebrity himself ....better known by sight than by acquaintance, and most frequently recognized as the driver of the two foreign cars he brought here with him. One is a Dusenberg of marked elegance, and the other of English make known as a Midget.

For amusement he prefers the companionship of some of the more rollicking beachboys, also seen aboard the Dusenberg, going places to have fun. His favorite seems to be Panama...he of the supreme nonchalance on a surfboard. Topping likes to watch Panama ride in backwards, standing on his head or doing numerous antics atop the waves. He likes to hear Panama sing funny songs, and see him play the clown. Panama plays the clown almost as well as he does the ukulele.

It is likely that the maharajah, mysterious and aloof, also preferred this novel and informal entertainment because until last Wednesday night he remained secluded, his presence in the city never suspected. Then Manager Fred Goodall of the Alexander Young Hotel received a reservation for dinner for ten persons, given by Henry J. Topping, Jr., in honor of the Maharajah of India....

The shining Dusenberg with its metal trimming rolled up to the door. With luxurious and neatly trimmed black beard, black silk turban, the real white dinner jacket of the Orient which the Occident has not quite been able to copy, the maharajah and his host, with some other guests, alighted and were escorted to their table.

The visitor fairly radiated with the elegance of the East. Those present at the roof-garden were agog. They watched from afar because that's as close as they could get. There was more whispering to the square yard than there had ever been before. The maharajah ate his excellent dinner quietly and paid little attention to his surroundings....

Spectators hoped he would dance so that they might dance past him and get a better look, but he sat quietly all evening, sipping champagne and conversing with others at the table....In fact, the presence of a member of Indian royalty caused such a stir that when the evening was over quite a crowd lingered in the lobby below to watch him leave, which he did with true dignity and maximum unconcern. But the crowd didn't see the tableau acted out in front of the waiting Dusenberg. There the maharajah paused and faced his host. "All right," he said. "I win the bet. Give me the twenty." He pulled off the turban, he pulled off the beard and there stood Panama. The distinguished visitor was nothing but a bet.*

It is not surprising that Panama was so popular with children. His high jinks made him seem a man permanently, albeit happily, stuck in adolescence, the beach his extended playground. Along with John ("Hawkshaw") Paia, a well-known surfboard stunt man, Panama used to teach children to play ukulele and make coconut hats. Panama used to say that he had taught two and even three generations of children from the same family to surf and that he was among the personal favorites of Red Skelton's nine-year-old son Richard.

Skelton made news in 1958 when he and his family unexpectedly arrived in Honolulu. Skelton had been in London, on the first leg of a planned around-the-world trip with his son, who was dying of leukemia, when a brutal British press accused him of capitalizing on his son's misfortune. Outraged, Skelton cut short his stay and headed for Hawaii. "It's my favorite place," he told the press. "It's Richard's, too, because he loves to surf and frolic with the beachboys."

P anama's childlike nature contributed to his popularity with women. Women said that he reminded them of a puppy. They seemed to want to adopt him, much as they might a pet. Among his greatest benefactors was Myrtle Swann, a Honolulu socialite who owned a lovely Spanish house overlooking the city that was a gathering place for beachboys on Sunday afternoons. Swann loved Panama and pampered him endlessly. She sent maids to clean his room, bought him clothes, and gave him money. When Panama needed a new set of false teeth, she paid for them. And whenever they got into a fight, she asked for them back. Their relationship continued for almost fifteen years. "Everybody thought they were going to get married," Panama's brother, John Baptiste, recalled. "And she was already married."

Like many beachboys, Panama was in no hurry to get to the altar. Once when asked if he had received many proposals, he replied, "Not one, but oodles. But when you marry rich people you get pressure. And you can have those movie-star girls. Look at how many divorces they have. You see your wife three months and they're on location nine months. Why does anyone marry a movie star?"

A lifeguard seems to be making sure Panama Dave obeys the sign as he takes a young woman out surfing. Photo courtesy of Charlie Lambert.

*An undated copy of this story, found in Panama Dave's scrapbook, is not listed in the newspaper index at the Hawaii State Library, nor is it in the subject index of the Hawaii Newspaper Agency. Knowledgeable sources believe it appeared in the late 1930s.

Panama was forty-five when he married Montana-born Patty Hutchinson. Hutchinson later recalled that she met Panama on the beach and that their courtship lasted three years. "He wanted to be sure he wanted a *haole*, and I wanted to be sure I wanted a *kanaka*," she told a reporter. "Then we got married."

It was, by all accounts, a successful marriage. The two were good for each other. But, inevitably, Patty got caught up in Panama's lifestyle and that was not good for either of them—especially Panama. By the mid-1960s, in his fifth decade on the beach, his drinking had taken a toll. "Toward the end, Panama was going down, down, down," Turkey recalled. "And he was getting skinny. That was from the drinking."

Kalei Holck, a beach attendant at the Royal Hawaiian, recalled being at the Moana's Kamaaina Bar one day when Panama's good friend, Doc Zimmerman, told him to drop his pants. Panama dropped his pants, and Zimmerman gave him a shot of vitamin B. Panama kept on drinking.

Not long afterward, the alcoholic hallucinations set in. "He'd be on the beach and yell, 'Duck! The blackbirds are here again,'" Holck recalled. "There were never any blackbirds."

Panama checked into Leahi Hospital on the slopes of Diamond Head, where one preliminary diagnosis seemed to indicate that he had tuberculosis. Then, his brother recalled, it was discovered that he had somehow obtained a tube of toy airplane glue. Deprived of alcohol, he had been sniffing the glue as a substitute.

In the spring of 1967, Panama was back on the beach. One April morning he went out to give a rare surfing lesson. His student that day, a young woman, later recalled that they were out in shallow water, 150 yards from shore, when he gave her board a push toward the beach. When she turned around he was gone. A short while later, a pair of servicemen saw his body floating by face down in the water. Panama was dead, felled by a heart attack at age fifty-seven.

An avid reader of obituaries, Panama predicted years before his death that his funeral would be the biggest Waikiki had ever seen. And it was. His passing was front-page news in the *Sunday Star-Bulletin and Advertiser*. In a fitting end to his improbable life, the story noted that not long after his body had been found at sea, the coconut hat he had always worn floated up on the beach.

Panama Dave having dinner at the Royal Hawaiian Hotel with actress Rosalind Russell. Photo courtesy of Charlie Lambert. (Opposite page) Panama Dave was forty-five before he married Montana-born Patty Hutchinson. Photo courtesy of the *Honolulu Star-Bulletin.*

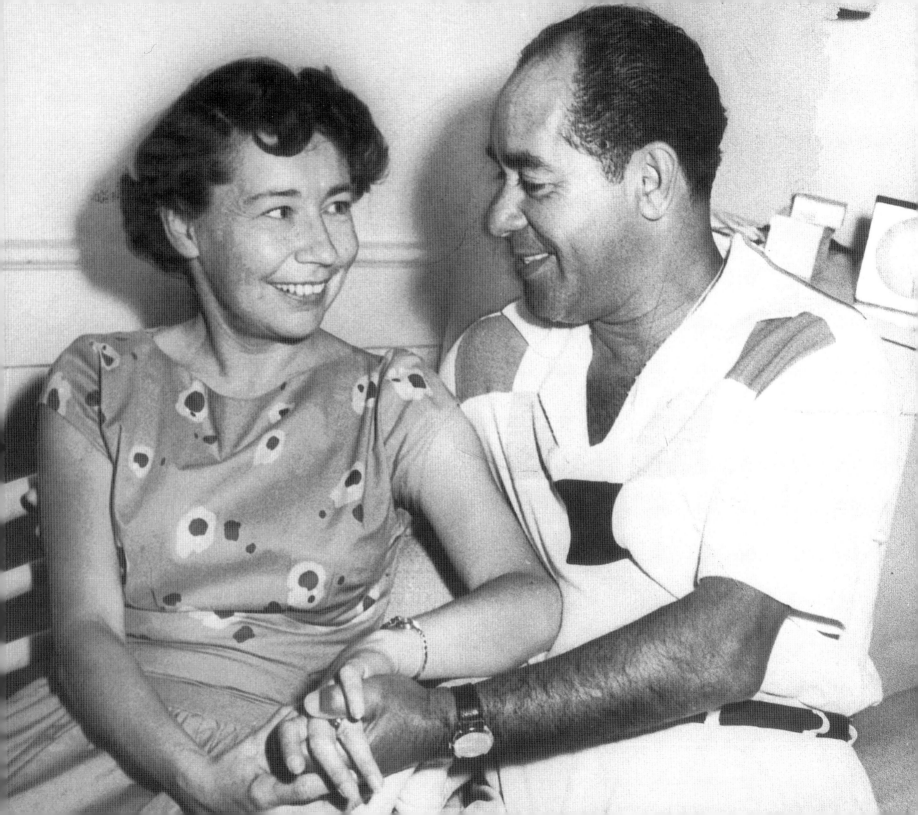

Harry Robello, a ruggedly handsome Portuguese beachboy, poses for an ad promoting surfing and romance at Waikiki. Photo circa 1940 courtesy of Harry Robello; hand-colored by Ron Hudson.

LIFE'S GREATEST PROFESSION
Of Liars and Lovers

7

Now she climbed back on the surfboard, and with Kelly instructing, started the long paddle out to catch the next wave, but when their board was well separated from the others, she relaxed backwards until she felt herself against the beachboy once more, and there she rested in his secure arms, paddling idly as his adept hands began their exploration beneath her new bathing suit. Sighing, she whispered, "Is this part of the standard instruction?"

—James Michener, *Hawaii*

James Michener's fictional character, Kelly Kanakaoa, confirmed what everyone wanted to believe about the Waikiki beachboy: that his real expertise was "estimating how long it would take him to get into bed with any newcomer." Michener forever branded the beachboy as a love'em-and-leave'em Hawaiian whose talents found a natural target in lonely, vacationing women. Kanakaoa, an expert surfer and slack-key guitarist, stood just over six feet and had jet-black hair and muscles "that rippled in the sunlight as if smeared with coconut oil." As a fictional character he made for good reading, but it remains uncertain whether or not his sexual prowess accurately reflects the sexual experiences of the Waikiki beachboys.

Harry Robello, a former beachboy, thinks not. "The beachboys lie like hell," he once told a writer. "Those days you didn't get anything—no way…but they all brag." Still, legend tells us otherwise. Beachboys remain a part of the romantic lore of Hawaii. They represent an interesting historical twist—the male counterpart to the tropical island maiden. In the same way that white men were attracted to dark-skinned girls, white women were drawn to the dark-skinned masculinity of the Waikiki beachboys. Or were they? How much of the legend is true?

Certainly, beachboys have always relished their role as sex objects. Turkey Love, who began his career as a beachboy in the 1930s, believes the beach can spoil a man. "Girlwise, moneywise—mostly girlwise—it's hard to break away," he said. Other beachboys, some active and well past fifty, claim they are still propositioned by women half their age. One remembered a woman who lost her bikini top during a surfing lesson and took his hand to cover her breast. "Let's get out of here," he whispered, and then paddled farther out and gratified her.

The beach has always acted as a powerful aphrodisiac; indeed, even today, one has only to walk along it to experience the excitement that is a part of every beachboy's daily existence. Sexual roles sometimes get reversed. One beachboy recalled standing inside a concession booth with two other beachboys when they were approached by a female tourist. Fixing her gaze on the first beachboy, the woman let her eyes travel slowly down his body, stopping at a point below the navel. Lifting her eyes to meet his, she smiled. The beachboy smiled back. Her gaze shifted to the second beachboy and, again, the routine was repeated. The third beachboy was standing in the shadows, beneath an umbrella, so that all the woman could see were his swim shorts illuminated by sunlight. Suddenly a voice seemed to be speaking to her from *inside* those shorts. "Take me," it said. "I'm on the pill."

No doubt sexual perquisites came with the profession. But was it always this way? Was it really this easy? Or, as Harry Robello claimed, do the beachboys exaggerate? To be sure, Waikiki has always been associated with romance, and in the years prior to the Second World War, its remoteness only added to the lure. Out in the surf, an ocean away, who would know?

Joe Akana on the beach in 1936 with a vocalist-dancer from a visiting musical. (Opposite page) With the romantic image of Diamond Head looming in the background, Sargent Kahanamoku makes a play for the woman of his fancy. Photos courtesy of Joe Akana.

Back then, both time and money were required to travel to the Islands. Those who could afford it were often seeking adventure or escaping the circumstances of their lives. "I came over on the *Lurline*," a woman from Reno, Nevada, recalled. "A divorce. I wanted to get out. In those days this was pretty far out." Not only was Hawaii an ocean away from the mainland, it was far removed from the mainland in terms of its sexual attitudes. Eugene Burdick, co-author of *The Ugly American*, noted in *The Blue of Capricorn*, a book published in 1961, that Polynesia was a place where sex had lost the element of guilt. "To the Westerner sex is a dramatic, committing, involving, often frightening thing," he wrote. "For the Polynesian it is a simple matter; as simple as eating or swimming or a prayer or an argument. It need not have consequences. It can be treated as an isolated moment of pleasure…holding no potential of guilt, no web of obligation, no need to murmur love words."

Hawaiians, of course, were among the first Polynesian people to adopt the Western concept of romantic love. Nevertheless, well into the twentieth century people were drawn to Hawaii by its sexual promise, and Hawaiians themselves retained a free and liberal sexual outlook. In a 1932 newspaper story, Hollywood screen star Dorothy Mackaill wrote that American women often lost all sense of moral balance in the Islands, going off with beachboys to luaus that sometimes lasted "several days."

It was easy to fall in love with a beachboy, and apparently many women did. A woman who came to Waikiki in the 1950s recalled the sand parties that took place even then, how in the evenings the beachboys would gather with their guitars and ukuleles and the divorcees would descend from their hotel rooms. As the sun dipped below the horizon and the moon rose over Diamond Head, they sang and laughed and fell in love. "Oh, the beachboys didn't fall in love," she said. "But those girls did. It was the way to mend a broken heart."

Grateful divorcees even established an informal referral system. A woman returning from the Islands would tell a friend, "Oh those Hawaiians down there, they're terrific!" And her friend in turn would write in advance or look up a beachboy when she arrived.

In fact, the beachboys were extraordinary. They were of exotic racial strains and many had excellent physiques. But not all of them were hunks. Far from it. Beachboys came in all shapes and sizes, and with all sorts of flaws. There is a story about a wealthy female tourist who talked endlessly about her beautiful, bronzed beachboy, Mystery. One day while having lunch with friends at the Royal Hawaiian Hotel, she spotted him out in the surf. "And there he is now," she exclaimed, "swimming in his ocean, swimming in his sea!" And, sure enough, there was Mystery, swimming. Suddenly, he dived down and came up with a

Chick Daniels, beach captain at the Royal Hawaiian Hotel, hams it up in a 1960s Sheraton publicity photo. Photo courtesy of Bobby Daniels.

handful of *limu* ("seaweed"), pulled out his false teeth, and proceeded to use the limu to clean them.

What was most appealing about the beachboys often had little to do with physical appearance. "Beachboys were people you wanted to sit and drink and laugh with," a Seattle woman recalled. "I was attracted by the independence. The go-to-hell attitude. The freedom." Cultural factors were also part of the attraction. Beneath its American veneer, Hawaii was very different. The people, the music, the food, and the fashions were all different. Falling in love with a beachboy was different, in part because he maintained a healthy disregard for Western sexual anxieties.

Beachboy songs were fraught with sexual innuendo. It is said that if tourists had truly understood the beachboys' songs, they would have got up and left. Instead, they clapped and sang along. Words like *okole* ("rear end") and *puka* ("opening," "hole") took on various shades of meaning. "Won't you teach me how to swim, how to swim, I'd like to swim with you," an old beach song, with accompanying movements, begins innocently. In succeeding verses, however, how to swim becomes how to hula and then how to *ami* ("wiggle the fanny") and finally how to "yeah."

Yeah?

"Yeah!" exclaimed beachboy Joe Akana. "That's the actual thing."

Make a woman laugh, especially about sex, and you con her in a special way, getting her to reveal a part of herself she may have forgotten about. The beachboys could do that. "The beachboys were lovers," recalled Squeeze Kamana, Jr., whose father, Squeeze, Sr., was a well-known beachboy musician. "They knew how to woo a woman—with their hands, with their eyes, with their words. They had the technique."

The beachboys also knew how to treat women well. Whether they had money or not, whether they were good looking or not, women sensed that the beachboys would take good care of them. "The beachboys were gentlemen," a California woman recalled. "A beachboy didn't make fun of you. He didn't abuse you. He didn't let anyone else abuse you. The women who came here loved the beachboys, and it was the way they were treated that kept bringing them back."

As popular with women as the beachboys may have been, they were frequently the bane of a hotel manager's existence. In general, the beachboys *were* well behaved, but when they were not the hotel was usually the first to know. For example, there was the beachboy who was discovered on a floor of a prominent Waikiki hotel where he should not have been. Attempting to escape, he jumped from a balcony to the top of a nearby coconut tree—and got caught.

As a rule, hotels did not allow beachboys above the lobby unless they were guests, but that rule was easily circumvented. Musicians would appear in their dress whites and say, "Musician!" as if they were going to a party, a change of clothes stashed inside their guitar cases. Access could also be obtained from desk clerks, bellhops, and doormen—lower-rung hotel employees with whom the beachboys were usually on good terms. In exchange for a share of gratuities or catches of fish, hotel employees would give beachboys information or look the other way.

Actress Leila Hyamas gets a *lomi lomi* massage from Sam Kahanamoku and husband Phil Berg. From the Hawaii State Archives. (Opposite page) During his younger days, Turkey Love (center) was a favorite among the ladies at Waikiki. Turkey is pictured here at Don the Beachcomber's with (at left) Harry Robello and a lady friend, and singer Alfred Apaka and his wife Edna. Photo courtesy of Harry Robello.

The avenues for sexual pursuit were many. At the Moana Hotel there was a fire escape and the door was always open. The night watchman was Tough Bill Keaweamahi. At the Royal Hawaiian it was no secret where the service elevators were located. "Hell, we used to live at the Royal," one beachboy boasted. "We were always sneaking up and making it with the girls. My friends and I used to say, 'Eh, by the time we get old we're going to have been laid in every room in this hotel.'"

Lomi lomi massage was another avenue of pursuit. This ancient Hawaiian practice, traditionally administered for therapeutic purposes with the hands and feet, often served instead as sexual foreplay, allowing a beachboy to get close to a woman. In the postwar years, beachboy Earl King had a discreet little place beneath the Outrigger Canoe Club where visitors could go for a massage. Prior to that, lomi lomi was often performed on the roof of the club, which was shaded from view by a giant hau tree.

Legend has it that the beachboys would take women up on the roof, peel their bathing suits back, put on the towels, and start applying coconut oil. Ox Keaulani recalled his technique: "I start 'round the neck, the arms, ribs, spine—I neva go near the rumpy parts—and pretty soon they start moaning. Then I go way down by the foot, start up. Pretty soon I'm getting close to *there*. My hand is like one lobster going for the puka. 'Stop!' she says. 'Stop?' 'Can we go up to my hotel room?' 'We go!'"

It was in the water, however, that the greatest number of sexual opportunities were realized. The water was warm and sensuous and acted as a giant curtain, screening from view everything beneath its surface. One beachboy advanced the theory that his profession's success with women had little to do with dark skin, handsome physiques, or engaging personalities. The real secret was the water.

The water?

"Wahines have a thing about it. Get a woman in the water and something happens. Every woman I ever met wanted to make love in the water. A lady once told me, 'When I was nineteen, you took me tandem. Can you imagine what is was like for me, going to a Catholic school on the mainland, to have a man take me surfing? To sit on top of me, on the back of my legs. The thrill I had. Skin to skin. In the water.'"

No doubt the sense of adventure of being far out from shore, alone with a beachboy on his surfboard, heightened sexual excitement. It is said that the beachboys used to get a surfboard, put beer inside a small, two-seater canoe, and take women way outside—where they would "swim, fool around, no bathing suit, nothing." Finally, they would make love to the women on the surfboard while other beachboys watched with binoculars from the beach.

Melvin Paoa, a first cousin to Duke Kahanamoku and a beachboy in the years prior to the Second World War, remembered well the things a beachboy could get away with in the water. Paoa, you may recall, was a notorious prankster, and he was especially devious in the water.

"Lot of tricks to surfing," he recalled, gazing out at the ocean one day at his home on the island of Molokai. "Like when you paddle tandem, your chest is always rubbing up against the wahine's okole. Let's say you lift up your chest little bit, so your *da kine* is on their okole. They might like that. And when you sit back on the board, sit way back, so the board tilts up and they slide back over you. Then you go lomi lomi

their legs or their shoulders. They could lose their bathing suit just by you rubbing them."

Paoa remembered that summers were the best times for sex. The winter tourist season brought an older crowd. The summers brought the coeds and the most adventurous women of all—the Canadian school teachers. After a day spent surfing, the beachboys would take them to a nightclub and make them drink fast so they would feel good. Then they would bring them back to the bar at the Moana. After that, if a beachboy was lucky, the woman would invite him up to her room, or he would try and talk her into going surfing. However, Paoa emphasized, "If you go in the water, you got to judge the wahine. Let's face it, if you're going moonlight surfing, you're not going for the surfing. But when you go at night, lot of tricks. Some of them don't swim so good, so you go where the breakers are—and let your board go. You know it's going wash up on the beach. Then they going hang on to you. They going grab you. Every damn thing. You let them hang on 'til they get tired. Same time you getting your cheap thrill. Good fun!"

To hear some beachboys tell it, their conquests at Waikiki were frequent and easy. And yet, not everyone remembered it that way. There are different perspectives on the sexual activities (actual or imagined) of the beachboys. Many remembered a different type of beachboy, one who was fun loving and friendly with strangers, inclined to be mischievous, occasionally a little naughty, but hardly the womanizer he has been made out to be. "You know what the old beach was like?" said Airedale McPherson, the window to the past opening in his mind. "I remember a girl, Frances was her name. Boy! Could she fill a bathing suit. I mean, yeah! She had a pair that stood up there as noble as Mount Haleakala. This was in the mid-1930s when fanny pinching started. That girl must have had a bruised right rectal cheek all her life."

Another, perhaps more telling, perspective on the beachboys' sexual activities comes from Harry Robello, who has called the entire legend into question. "What you're seeing now is not like before," he said. "You didn't buy a woman breakfast and get lucky. No way. The beachboys had to be straight-line. Well mannered. Women were safe with the beachboys."

Robello recalled that Matson, which owned the Royal Hawaiian and Moana hotels, was a lot stricter than some care to remember. A beachboy could not risk making a play for a woman in the water for fear of being reported to the hotel. There was also a racial stigma attached to being Hawaiian: "You a brown boy, get little bit dark skin, you stay away." If a girl asked a beachboy for information about a good nightspot, he might tell her where to go, even meet her there, but he did not dare ask her out. "She tell her parents, her parents tell the hotel, you out."

Robello and others like him imply that the womanizing beachboy is a creature of Michener's imagination. The beachboys have merely acquiesced to fiction, perhaps all too aware that their mystique depends on it. Time, of course, is on their side; legends grow with the years. Moreover, human nature is such that sexual myths are easy to exploit. Add to this a lesson beachboys learned long ago: that when a man with dark skin is seen with a white woman it is almost always assumed that he is sleeping with her. In fact, this may or may not be the case.

Take, for example, tobacco heiress Doris Duke, who was an admirer of the beachboys and a great friend of Sam Kahanamoku. Opinion was always divided on the beach as to whether Doris and Sam were friends or lovers. Sam was Doris's caretaker at Shangri-la. He lived downstairs near the pool. Doris lived upstairs in the main house, and as a result there were always rumors that the two were carrying on. People even started calling him Sam Cromwell because at that time she was Doris Duke Cromwell.

The role of escort and companion—not lover—was a more common one for a beachboy. Robello was once quoted as saying, "You take all the beachboys, maybe two guys would get lucky [with a female tourist] ....One person score twice a year he's lucky. Some guys no score for five years, I tell you. The beachboys weren't that lucky."

By casting a shadow on the legend, it has been suggested that Robello is trying to bring the myth into balance. But as one writer put it, "By throwing in the element of doubt, he further enhances the mystique." However, when beachboy talk turns to women, and to men who were successful with women, Robello's name always comes up. Pictures show him to have been ruggedly handsome, a Portuguese with fair skin. He was also smart, one of the few beachboys who became financially successful. One fellow beachboy recalled that women used to "fight over Harry."

As Turkey Love tells it, one of the few women he ever lost was to Robello. "Back in the old days," Turkey recalled, "when tourists came to the office to get a surfing lesson, we had names on this board. When the guy ahead of you got called, you slipped your name on top. And when your name was called, you slipped it back down on the bottom. One

morning Lana Turner came up for a surfing lesson. Wow! What a good-looking woman. She was about eighteen and just becoming a star. I was twenty-five and in my prime. And second on the list. Robello got her."

Many other beachboys were also reputed womanizers. Duke Kahanamoku is said to have had his fun during his years in Hollywood, Chick Daniels was dubbed "the doctor" for his touch with the ladies, and Rabbit Kekai, who did not drink or smoke, was not known to place other restrictions on himself.

Who was the all-time, leading ladies man on the beach? Turkey Love is certainly a candidate. The beachboy for Henry J. Kaiser and the brother of Winona Love, a renowned Hawaiian hula dancer, Turkey was tall, charismatic, and charming. Among his girl friends were Lammie Lucas, stepdaughter of millionaire Chris Holmes, and Jane Harding, daughter of actress Ann Harding. Turkey recalled that Harding was very fond of him but that he never took the relationship seriously because he was having too much fun. "I used to be fond of this other girl, and I found out later that her family owned a whole town in California," he said. "I found that out twenty years later. Read it in a magazine. But I never thought of that

Tobacco heiress Doris Duke returns to Shangri-la, her $2 million fantasy retreat at Diamond Head, escorted by Sam Kahanamoku (right) and his brother David. From the Hawaii State Archives.

To Steamboat —
with very best wishes from
Deborah Kerr

While filming a motion picture in Hawaii in the early 1950s, actress Deborah Kerr goes for an outrigger canoe ride with Steamboat Mokuahi. Photo courtesy of Steamboat Mokuahi.

back then, the money part of it, how rich they were and all that. I was having too much fun."

One wonders, though, if the beachboys were not more calculating. Beachboy recollections of the past are not without contradictions. Money may not have been important if a woman had it, but what about women like the Canadian school teachers who did not? "Oh yeah, the teachers," said one beachboy. "They came during the summers. I usually looked for women who were staying at the Royal Hawaiian Hotel. I was looking for the money part of it. Sex later. The school teachers didn't have money."

Women with money were, for some beachboys, prized conquests; indeed, the modern notion of a beachboy is less of a gentleman and more of a gigolo. Were the beachboys hired lovers? Some admit they were, and that older women were their favorites.

A number of beachboys married women with money, although not necessarily for their money. Beachboy musician Charlie Amalu, for example, wed an heiress to the Estate of James Campbell, one of the Islands' largest landholders. And Melvin Paoa's second wife was an heiress to the landed Kaumakani Estate on Molokai. French-Tahitian-Hawaiian beachboy Barry Napoleon, who began his career in the 1950s, married and later divorced a Wells Fargo heiress.

But perhaps the most unusual story concerns Buster Jeremiah. Jeremiah was an ace ukulele player and a talented surfer who worked on the beach in front of the Royal Hawaiian Hotel. In the mid-1950s, he married a mainland heiress whose estimated worth was more than a million dollars. Soon after, he moved to the mainland and began enjoying the good life. He bought expensive cars and shoes and indulged his passion for gambling. A friend who knew him then estimated that Jeremiah took him on dozens of junkets and that it was not uncommon for him to walk into a bar with five-thousand dollars in his wallet and offer to take a party of ten to Las Vegas.

Jeremiah's spending continued unabated until, after about ten years, he had used up the better part of his wife's fortune. Somehow the marriage survived. In fact, Jeremiah had three children by the heiress, and at the time of their thirtieth anniversary, the two were still together—living on Hawaiian Homestead land on the island of Hawaii. "I was a fool with my wife's money," Jeremiah once confessed to a friend. "But I always loved her."

Most beachboys did eventually marry, and perhaps because it signaled such a drastic change in lifestyle, their weddings were often memorable occasions. In the summer of 1957, Ernest ("Mud") Werner married Bettie Monroe of Los Angeles in a ceremony that began a half-mile from shore. A newspaper account of the event said that the bride and bridegroom rode down "the watery aisle" on separate catamarans emblazoned with blue, white, and yellow sails. Mud's catamaran beached first, unloading a dozen lei-bedecked beachboys dressed in lava-lavas. They sang as they carried coconut-frond baskets of fruit ashore.

Monroe's catamaran followed, discharging a dozen girls in muumuus and pink-carnation leis who escorted the bride to the minister. When the ceremony concluded, the newlyweds strolled up the beach to a fabulous reception. More than eight hundred guests drank champagne from coconut half shells, conical sea shells, and calabashes at a party that lasted into the next morning.

Mud's marriage to Monroe did not work out, however; beachboy marriages to mainland wahines seldom did. Henry Kim, the University of Hawaii sociology student who in 1966 wrote his master's thesis on the Waikiki beachboy, noted that of the twenty-four beachboy marriages he examined only eight remained stable. Factors common to all of the successful marriages were wives who were born and raised in Hawaii and children. "The greatest incidence of marital breakup appears in marriages between beachboys and young Caucasian women from the mainland," he concluded.

That is hardly surprising. The beach did not provide a stable source of income, and the temptations were many. Mainland women, wracked by suspicion and jealousy, were often adamant that their husbands take up another profession. But a beachboy who quit the beach often could not adjust to life off it. And those who went to the mainland with their wives often felt like cultural misfits. A friend of Buster Jeremiah recalled the first time Jeremiah sat down to a coat-and-tie dinner with his wife's family. A waiter placed a plate of chicken and a finger bowl in front of him, and he picked up the finger bowl and drank from it. He thought it was miso soup.

Mainland women who stayed in Hawaii did not always adjust, either. One woman recalled that she saw "too many of the haole girls going down the tubes quick—drinking too much, getting fat, not getting up until noon." Local women were more tolerant of their men, but they, too, had problems. Some spoke with bitterness of men who squandered their paychecks, drank too much, brought home friends at all hours of the night, and were unfaithful. "Beachboys don't know how to settle down," said the former wife of one beachboy. "They're like musicians. Their marriages never work."

The sad fact is that even the majority of beachboys who had long marriages eventually got divorced. Squeeze Kamana, Jr., who spent a few years as a beachboy himself, said that his father was one of the few who realized that the beach and marriage were a bad combination. When Squeeze, Sr., stopped being a bachelor, he stopped being a beachboy. "Dad told me there comes a time when you have to get off the beach. He said you can always go back. The beach will always be there. For a lot of guys who stayed on the beach, that was their life. They never wanted to change. They never wanted to get off the beach. A lot of them didn't grow up. They stayed on the beach. Struggled on the beach. Got married. Got divorced. They couldn't divorce themselves from the beach to take care of their families."

Getting off the beach was never easy. For Harry Robello's generation it took a declaration of war. "If not for the war, I think not one beachboy would have left," he said. "I doubt it." The lifestyle was too good. The sun, the surf, the parties, and especially the women. Michener may have exaggerated the beachboys' predatory sex habits, and the beachboys may have done some embellishing themselves, but the evidence suggests that they fared better than most. It is not surprising that some beachboys got spoiled. But for all the beautiful women they enjoyed, not many were able to keep one. When the party was over, a lot of them woke up and found that they were growing old alone.

Colgate Nawai bids aloha to a friend on Boat Day. (Opposite page) Splash Lyons (left), Tough Bill Keaweamahi (back right), and Chick Daniels on the beach in 1929 with a pair of Australian lasses. Photos courtesy of Joe Akana.

During his fifty years as head beachboy at the Royal Hawaiian Hotel, Chick Daniels handed out towels, umbrellas, and advice. Photo courtesy of Joe Daniels; hand-colored by Ron Hudson.

CHICK DANIELS
The Happiest Hawaiian

8

Chick always answered his phone, I'm ready,…
—Michael McPherson, *Beachboy*

It has been said that in the pursuit of money the Polynesian is irresponsible; in the pursuit of happiness, dedicated. Whether or not it is true, this adage speaks volumes about Waikiki's most celebrated beachboy, Chick Daniels. But it also suggests a disquieting paradox: how can a life fully lived seem to have been squandered?

Beachboys who knew Chick always said that he *could've been a millionaire*. Some said it with wide-eyed amazement and others with a twinge of envy, for Chick made and spent a fortune, and had a good time doing it. "Chick had to have fun with his money," recalled his old sidekick, Turkey Love. "He showed me one time, in one week in tips he made two-thousand dollars. That's like twenty-thousand dollars now. He hired a plane and took six of us to Molokai. We opened up a bar, drank, came back. That was Chick Daniels. He made it and he threw it away."

In a world obsessed with accumulating money, Chick was obsessed with spending it. As head beach attendant at the Royal Hawaiian Hotel, he had the money job, and he had the personality to exploit it. Hawaiians said that Chick was *kolohe*, or "crazy." Not crazy as in nuts but "wild-kind crazy—good fun."

"You want to know about Chick Daniels?" said John D. Kaupiko, grandson of the famous beachboy who had the same name. John D. recalled a scene at the Los Angeles airport in 1952, when he was returning home from college. He was standing in a ticket line, and across the terminal he saw a baggage porter coming toward him. The porter was making his way through a crowd, and there was "this half-crazed guy" riding in his handcart. Suddenly, John D. realized who it was.

"Uncle Chick!"

"Young John D.!"

Chick was wearing shorts, a tanktop, and no shoes. He also was out of his mind. He had been drinking. He wanted to give John D. some money, but he did not even have a wallet.

"What are you doing here, Uncle Chick?"

"I've been kidnapped! Young John D. I went to see this wahine off at the airport, and she told me she was taking me with her on the plane."

For the greater part of his eighty-three years, Chick Daniels was toasted by celebrities who carried his name, and sometimes his person, back to Hollywood. He led the beachboy's life, and he led it to the hilt. But in the end that life rose up and struck him like a surfboard from behind. The beachboy who could not go broke ended up a broken man. Perhaps there is a message here. Perhaps there also is a message in his madness. Certainly no beachboy ever had as much fun, spent as much money, or was as well loved as Chick Daniels.

A playful Chick bites into a huge *mahi mahi,* or dolphin. Hawaiians said that Chick was *kolohe,* or crazy. Not crazy as in nuts, but "wild-kind crazy—good fun." Photo courtesy of Bobby Daniels. (Opposite page) Chick (without shirt) was always a focal point at any gathering. Here, he entertains friends at a beachside bar. Photo courtesy of Jim McMahon.

Even while quietly strumming a ukulele, Chick had a distinctive flair. Photo courtesy of Bobby Daniels.

F ew men are so charismatic as to define an era, to have their birth coincide with its beginning, their death mark its passing. William ("Chick") Daniels was such a man. Chick Daniels was born in 1899 to German-Hawaiian parents and raised on the island of Kauai.* He went to school until the ninth grade, and in his nineteenth year was drafted on the last call of the First World War. Two weeks later the armistice was signed, and Chick was spared. "They knew I was coming," he used to joke.

He took a job at the Honolulu Iron Works as a machinist's helper. The year was 1919, the pay was three dollars a day, and the workers called a strike. Chick's cousin, Hiram Anahu, persuaded him to come down to the beach, and once he tasted the lifestyle he never left.

The story goes that there was already a Steamboat Bill, a Tough Bill, and a Bill Kahanamoku at Waikiki, so the other beachboys started calling him "Chick" after a popular movie detective. The name fit, although it took on a different personality when he wore it. "Chick" Daniels was not a sleuth but a swashbuckler.

The many sides of his character found full expression on the beach. Chick was a strong swimmer who liked to surf and spearfish. He was also a consummate entertainer; an aunt who was a music teacher schooled him when he was young. He played ukulele, danced a wicked hula, and had a deep, rich, soulful voice.

His real talent, however, was with people. People could not get enough of Chick or he of them. A columnist once wrote that it was easy to get to know Chick Daniels—all you had to do was ask him for a towel. On the beach in front of the Royal Hawaiian, he had a shack where he stored backrests and a bench nearby where he sat, accessible to all. He was a big man, long limbed and barrel chested, and his presence lit up the beach. "People just sort of gravitated to Chick," one long-time visitor recalled. "He always had a story to tell, a song to sing. He had his uke and he'd be entertaining and singing around. He had that happy personality."

Honolulu Star-Bulletin columnist William Drury once noted that Chick was an institution at Waikiki, his chatty hospitality drawing a constant parade of visitors to his bench. One day in 1960 Drury paused at Chick's bench himself. He wrote this account:

"Hello," [Chick] said, coming forward to greet me. "When did you get back?" He knew my face but had forgotten my name, and naturally assumed I was one of the thousands who come and go year after year. "When did you get back?" is a question Chick Daniels must have asked thousands of times.

*Daniels used to say that he was Irish Hawaiian. However, his daughter, Mary Lee Makalena, said that a genealogical study done of the family revealed otherwise.

Our conversation was constantly interrupted by pink, paunchy gentlemen in scanty beach attire. One carried a miniature transistor radio which ceaselessly chattered about a football battle between the New York Giants and the Baltimore Colts. He appeared every 15 minutes or so to give Daniels the latest results of the game.

"Giants 9 to 7," he said, coming up for the third or fourth time.

Chick said, "Right."

The man ambled away.

"He's a big surplus dealer on the continent," said Chick....

The surplus dealer came back. "Baltimore just scored," he said.

"Colts 14 to 9."

"Right," said Chick....

Another paunchy gentleman came up and joined us on Chick's bench. The man mentioned Maui. "Maui?" said Chick. "I'll tell you about Maui. I went there once with Esther Williams and Jane Russell. We were in this hotel. There were horses' heads all along the wall behind the bar. Horses' heads, everywhere you looked. Outside they had a big pasture. And not a horse in sight."

The man left. "Twenty years ago he was here," said Chick. "Twenty years, that's a long time. I knew him then."

He started to tell me about the Shah of Iran and Ray Milland and Gregory Peck and Arthur Godfrey, but kept breaking off to hand out towels and backrests.

"Do you lose many towels?" I asked.

"Thousands," he said. "People steal 'em. "Got R. H. on 'em, for Royal Hawaiian...."

A third paunchy man appeared. "Chick," he said, "I didn't get to say good-bye the last time I was here."

"Don't worry about it," said Daniels, slapping him on the shoulder.

When the man had gone, Chick said, "He owns a restaurant in San Francisco. Comes here six or seven times a year...."

A fourth pink paunchy gentleman arrived at the bench, in search of an umbrella. Chick greeted him amiably.

"When did you get back?" he asked.

The man looked puzzled.

"This is my first trip."

A twist to Chick Daniels' happy-go-lucky demeanor was that he was a man easily given to sentimentality. He was also fastidious. Beachboys who worked with or near Chick all recalled that he was a strict disciplinarian. When he worked, he worked hard. "He wanted things done right," said Charlie Lambert, an attendant with the adjacent Outrigger Beach Services in the 1950s. "You were well groomed.

You were polite. You smiled." Each morning Chick and his crew put chairs and towels out for hotel guests and were there all day attending to their needs. Chick himself carried the towels over his arm like a *maitre d'*, laying them down for guests so that "the sand fit their fanny." Guests had four towels to each chair. And two cushions.

Chick's most important attribute, however, was his vitality. Veteran Outrigger Canoe Club member Chris Cusack, who first met Chick in 1927, recalled that it was as if he had the energy and charm of two men. Chick was always in motion. When he was not entertaining and singing, he was marching up and down the sand, laughing, joking, talking it up.

And then there would come a time each day after the beach emptied out when Chick would take off his tank top and change from his khaki shorts into his swimming trunks. "It was almost a ritual," said Cusack. "He would run—and every beachboy I ever knew never walked into the water. They would run and duck their neck and curl their shoulders and hit the water, come up, swim all around. For Chick, it was sort of an exuberant thing, like his personality. Then he'd go shower, come out in maybe gray flannels, nice tasseled slippers, a blazer, wink and say, 'Got a big date tonight.' And off he'd go."

A snappy dresser and consummate entertainer, Chick never failed to delight tourists when he launched into one of his many hulas. Photo courtesy of Bobby Daniels. (Opposite page) In a scene that captures the joy and spontaneity of a beachboy party, Chick cuts loose with his "cocktail shake" hula. Also participating in the festivities are (front row from left) Coconut Willie Cohen, Panama Dave, bass player Mystery Cockett, guitarist Melvin Paoa, Duke Kahanamoku, and Kalakaua Aylett. Seated on the sand with a towel around his neck is Jimmy Hakuole. Photo courtesy of Charlie Lambert.

W hen the beach closed up, Chick headed for the bars. The Barefoot Bar, Don the Beachcomber's, and Tiki Torch were among his many haunts, although his favorite place was called the Palm Tree Inn. Except for the people who frequented it, there was nothing special about the Palm Tree Inn. It was a little hideaway bar toward the west end of Waikiki, popular with the beach crowd. On afternoons when it rained, Chick led the chorus, "It's Palm Tree time!"

Chick was always a focal point at the Palm Tree, as indeed he was at any bar or party. He would get up and move a potted plant next to his table, saying, "I need some shade." He would slip off his watch and drop it in a stranger's drink. Winking at his victim, he would say, "Just checking your timing." At tourist gatherings when the host said, "Ladies and gentlemen, we have a famous beachboy with us tonight from the Royal Hawaiian Hotel!" Chick would get up and drop his pants.

His pants-dropping act, which could come at the climax of any one of his many hulas, was not lewd or offensive, but it frequently shocked the uninitiated. Chick would loosen his belt buckle, cross his arms, and begin swinging his hips—'round and 'round—until his pants slid down to his ankles to reveal polka-dotted or striped underwear.

The pants-dropping hula became identified with Chick during his career as an entertainer. That career spanned some forty years and began its ascent in 1925 when, on his first trip to the mainland, he performed with the Los Angeles Philharmonic as part of a Hawaiian opera, *Pele and Lohiau*. When the Royal Hawaiian Hotel opened in 1927, Chick formed his own troupe, the Royal Hawaiians. For more than ten years he played at cocktail parties, dinners, and late-evening dances, although perhaps his finest moment occurred when the Royal Hawaiian had its opening. As Princess Abigail Kawananakoa stepped up to be the first to sign the register, Chick burst into "Hawaii Ponoi," prompting the princess and everyone else to join in the singing.

A big baseball fan, Chick went to the World Series eight years in a row with millionaire Ed Bennecke. Photo courtesy of Bobby Daniels.

Chick made his second trip stateside in 1929. A planned voyage to the South Seas had been called off because of the stock-market crash, so Chick accepted the invitation of Montana copper magnate William Clarke and traveled to Hollywood to play with the Biltmore Trio, which performed in supper clubs and on radio. Clarke was one of many wealthy men with whom Chick forged close relationships. In the early 1930s, millionaire Chris Holmes hired him as a companion and as caretaker for his palatial seaside estate at Queen's Surf. Chick subsequently worked in a similar capacity for millionaire Bob Topping, whose home near Diamond Head featured a sixty-foot slide that swung from the terrace to the swimming pool below.

Like Panama Dave, Chick was popular with rich men because he kept them laughing and at ease. He also was a philosopher who handed out backrests, towels, and advice. "The way to stay young is to relax all the time," he would tell them. "You people don't have a life. You have a schedule. If you take a day off, you don't know what to do with yourself. Take a day off! Break the schedule!"

More instructive, though, was his attitude toward money. Chick was that rare individual who taught the rich how to enjoy wealth. When he sat down with his millionaire friends, he outspent them. He always picked up the check. In part, he was demonstrating his hospitality, but he also knew that sometime in the future the favor would be returned. For Chick the payoff came on boat days, when he reaped huge tips.

Still, by any standard, Chick was exceedingly generous. He had trouble entering a bar without buying drinks for the house, and he was forever lending money to his beach buddies, buying them drinks, and taking them on trips. "Chick's money was from day to day," recalled Harry Robello. "At no time did he have a bank account, that's for sure. If he made one-thousand dollars today, it would be gone tomorrow."

Chick's relationship with money—how he made it, how he spent it—was a continuing source of fascination. A good chair on his beach, for instance, carried the same prestige as a ringside seat at a prizefight. Accordingly, there was a section where his favorites sat, and then there was "Siberia," a remote section way off in the corner where he sent those whom he did not like or who did not tip.

But Chick was also discriminating about whom he gave money to. It is said that when he stayed at a hotel he would leave a five-dollar bill as bait on the dresser. If it disappeared, he wrote room service a note when he checked out that read: "THANK YOU AND MAHALO." Honesty received a more substantial gratuity.

How could someone who was so obviously *akamai* ("smart") about money also be so reckless? Kalei Holck, a musician and former beach attendant at the Royal Hawaiian Hotel, theorized that Chick "hated" money. "When you spent it like he did, you had to hate it," he said. "If you like money, you can't be close to a millionaire." Holck recalled that Chick kept a large container at the beach into which he threw his small change. It was mostly silver dollars, but it added up. "When he had about seven-hundred dollars, you could see he was getting nervous," said Holck. "He's like a volcano. He's got money. He has to spend it. And then bam! He's gone for three or four days. When he comes back, he's okay."

To curb his compulsion to spend, Chick had friends hold his money. Others tried to get him to invest some of his money, but Chick was never interested. "That bugga could have been a millionaire *twice* if he would have saved his money," Molokai Horner recalled. "But you could never get Chick to save a dime.

He would have to blow it." Harry Robello recalled asking him one time, "Chick, how come you no save?" Said Chick, "Well, you know, the more you give, the more you get." That was his philosophy.

Chick no doubt realized at a certain point in his life what he had squandered, but according to friends, he had few, if any, regrets. "He didn't kick himself for what he could have bought, what he might have had," said Charlie Lambert. "I always hated it when people said, 'I've never seen anyone spend so much money so quickly as Chick.' It had the wrong connotation. He was just a generous man, a giving man. There's a difference between those who are too free with their money and those who want to have fun with it."

C hick Daniels was not one to fear for his financial security. Life for him was something to be lived, not something to be collected and left behind. Money was the fuel that kept the good times rolling. Not surprisingly, people admired this attitude and celebrated his excesses. Acts others might have had a hard time getting away with—diving into a fishpond while having lunch with Arthur Godfrey, for instance, or arriving by rickshaw at an exclusive Waikiki restaurant outfitted in a safari suit and hat—were, when they involved Chick, readily accepted.

His shortcomings were just as easily overlooked. Not only was he a big spender, he was a big drinker who could be *pilikia* ("trouble") when he had too much. He was also something of a philanderer. While working for Chris Holmes in 1934, he was arrested and fined one-hundred dollars for conducting "petting parties" with an eighteen-year-old girl in his Waikiki apartment.

"Oh, he was a wild one all right," said beachboy Joe Akana, recalling a time in 1929 when Chick took care of a group of stockbrokers vacationing in Waikiki. Akana saw Chick driving them home one morning in a Packard Twin-Six. They came roaring by wearing nothing but sheets. "Do you know where Chick had taken them?" he said. "The brothel. And they had wives, too."

Chick, in fact, fathered five children. He had two sons by his first wife, Ann Noa, and two daughters and a son by his second wife, Violet Ornellas, a young hula dancer who was half his age when they met in 1931 during the filming of *Bird of Paradise*.

To the credit of his wives, both marriages were fairly lengthy, the second enduring for twenty-five years. At one point, he even bought a house, only to find that making payments on something that did not yield a good time was, for him, an exercise in futility. As much as Chick loved his family, the lure of the beach was stronger than his resolve to divorce himself from its lifestyle.

In the end, both women divorced him. Chick was not one to bring his money home, and he often did not himself come home. He would take off, and his wife often had to learn of his whereabouts in the newspaper. Squeeze Kamana, Jr., who was related to Chick, remembered running into Chick on a return flight from a 1952 mainland college-football game. In those days, the crossing took twelve hours, and

"People just sort of gravitated to Chick," one longtime visitor recalled. "He always had a story to tell and a song to sing. He had his uke and he'd be entertaining and singing around. He had that happy personality." Photo courtesy of Bobby Daniels.

about half way out Squeeze realized that there were no stewardesses. "Up front I could hear all this partying and singing going on," he said, "so I walked up the aisle to nose around. When I got up to the front, there were Chick and Turkey. One stewardess was in Chick's lap, the other in Turkey's. Chick had on an English bobby's helmet, shorts, tank top, no shoes. The same clothes he had left in, he was coming back in. Later, I ran into his wife at the airport. Chick had just up and gone without telling her. That's how he was. No responsibility."

With the coming of commercial air service to the Islands after the war, Chick was increasingly absent from the beach. In 1950, Arthur Godfrey brought him to New York to perform on his national radio and television programs. Chick stayed a month, flying with Godfrey to his Pennsylvania farm, to Florida, to Washington, and back to New York.

During the 1950s, Chick played bit parts in several films, including *Mr. Roberts* and *The Old Man and the Sea*. Mike Mullahey, whose father started Waikiki's main beach service at the Outrigger Canoe Club, recalled that about three or four times a year the phone would ring on the beach, and it would be one of Chick's friends from Hollywood. "He'd say, 'Look, I'm going to throw a party here tomorrow night, and I need a couple of you guys to bring some beach towels. Just go down to the airport and there will be a ticket waiting for you.' And Chick and Panama would go down, each with a load of beach towels, and fly first class to L.A. A limousine would meet them at the airport, and they'd be whisked away to spend a week or ten days in the absolute lap of luxury."

By the time jet service started up in the 1960s, Chick was traveling to Tahiti and Tokyo with Turkey Love and Ed Bennecke, a millionaire who made his money manufacturing toilet seats. Turkey recalled that one night on the Ginza a band broke into a Hawaiian number and Chick got up and dropped his pants. "And he didn't have any underwear on, too," he said. Bennecke's family was part owner of Schlitz beer, which sponsored major-league baseball games, and for eight straight years he took Chick and Turkey to the World Series. They would travel to both cities and see all the games.

But Bennecke died in 1968. Duke Kahanamoku died that same year (Panama Dave had passed away in 1967), leaving Chick, who was approaching seventy, a remnant of the old guard. Although he was still beach captain at the Royal Hawaiian, his absences from work had become a concern. Sheraton was faced with a dilemma: how do you fire a legend? Chick's conduct on the beach was impeccable, and he was as popular as ever with guests. But he was rarely around. Harry Robello, who was then operating the other Sheraton concessions, recalled what happened when Sheraton tried to fire Chick.

"Chick, you're through," said the manager.

"I ain't through," said Chick. "You can't fire me." He grabbed the phone and started calling some of his big-name friends. "Here, they want to talk to you."

The manager went to the phone. Chick was rehired on the spot.

According to Robello, Sheraton finally offered him another job as greeter, which required him to meet VIPs at the airport. "Chick would have been perfect for that job," he said. "But he refused it. Then they

Chick and his second wife, Violet Ornellas, whom he met during the filming of *Bird of Paradise* in 1931, were married for twenty-five years. Photo courtesy of Bobby Daniels.

said, 'Well, we can't leave you on the beach 'cause you're never there.' So Chick took his money and retired."

Some saw Chick's departure as sad but inevitable. Charlie Lambert recalled that Chick cried at first, perhaps feeling the cumulative loss. A man does not end an association of more than fifty years and not feel it.

The party that had begun in 1927 at the Royal Hawaiian was over. The big tippers, the boats, the old haunts, and the old friends were quickly disappearing, if they were not already gone. Chick was slow to accept it. "Chick didn't like progress," said Lambert. "He didn't accept change. When they tore down the Palm Tree, he slept in his car in the parking lot for two weeks. It was as if he was conducting a vigil."

Chick's enthusiasm for life never diminished, but his income did. He moved from a neighborhood on the outskirts of Waikiki to an apartment near the beach. A state subsidy covered his rent, but otherwise he was living on social-security payments and a retirement income of sixty dollars a month. He rose every morning before dawn and, seeking companionship, would call his friends. Drunk one night, he took a dare and married a taxi driver whom he had known for only twelve hours. The marriage was annulled the next day when he sobered up and discovered that she had stolen his car.

Still, Chick had the beach. He went for a swim every morning, and old clients still left him envelopes filled with cash. His close friend Andrea Cassidy, a wealthy and beautiful divorcee who had been coming to Waikiki since the early 1950s, set up a small trust fund for him. It was not much, she admitted, only a hundred dollars a month. "I just wanted him to have a little go-to-hell money," she said.

Cassidy called Chick every week from her home in Reno. In the mid-1970s, after Chick had survived a pair of heart attacks, her calls became more frequent. One day she called and Chick was not in his apartment. She called his favorite bar, and he was not there either, and she knew that he could not be anywhere else.

"It happened just like I knew it was going to happen," she said. "I kept telling everyone that he's going to be up in that apartment, and we're not going to find him. Sure enough, he laid up there how long? Eight hours before they found him? The water was running and it started going underneath the door. It was too long. And, of course, everybody who knew him wished he had gone right then. After that, he knew you, but that was it."

Chick Daniels spent the last five years of his life in a convalescent home, the victim of a stroke. It was not a place you would have wanted to visit; in fact, many of Chick's closest friends did not, preferring to remember him as he had once been. Shortly before Chick's death in 1982, Harry Robello told a writer, "It's all over the day Chick goes." And, indeed, when his ashes were scattered at sea in September of that year, an era that had long since passed came to an official end.

Relatives and friends probably told Chick Daniels stories that day, stories about the crazy things he did and said, and about the way he had made and spent his money. But no one expressed sadness about the way he had lived his life, only about the way it had ended. "Everybody met a lot of millionaires on the beach," said Charlie Lambert. "But there was only one Chick." He was one in a million.

At Chick's 1982 beach-boy funeral in Waikiki, an era that had long since passed officially came to an end. Photo by Brett Uprichard.

This oil painting of Scooter Boy Kaopuiki was on display during his 1985 beachboy funeral at Waikiki. Photo by Grady Timmons.

BEYOND THE REEF
Requiem for a Beachboy

9

Out where the blue water begins, in that deep azure where in the sunlight you can see the reef falling away and sometimes even the sudden silver flash of a bottom feeder turning, out past the hundred foot hole holding Kui's bones, way out there Chick them are doing the backstroke into their golden years.

—Michael McPherson

Few places have changed so much in so short a time as Waikiki. A unique stretch of beach that was once exclusive has become overcrowded. The aloha spirit that was once authentic has become commercialized. Ocean liners have been replaced by jumbo jets that bring more people with less money. Although Diamond Head and two marvelous old hotels still stand, the shoreline and the skyline have been significantly altered.

For all this, however, it is hard to separate the place from the past. Fishermen still patiently ply the surf. Outrigger canoes still shuttle back and forth. Surf riders still slide across the waves silhouetted against the afternoon sun. The old values and the old ways may be gone, but the ocean remains. For a beachboy, it is the one constant, the one thing he knows he can go back to.

For as long as anyone can remember, beachboys have been returning to the ocean as a last rite, a final resting place. Exactly when the practice began is not clear, but most likely an early beachboy made the request and others, struck by the appropriateness of the ceremony, continued the tradition.

Over the years, the ceremony developed its own ritual. Beachboy Joe Akana, a licensed mortician who has arranged most of beachboy burials at sea since the 1930s, recalled that in the old days he used to take up a collection among the beachboys to pay for the service. At a precise hour, he had the urn delivered to him on Kalakaua Avenue. From there, he led a procession down to the beach where a flotilla of canoes waited. A short beachside service followed. A minister delivered the last rites, and then those assembled sang the decedent's favorite songs, concluding with "We Love You, Hui Nalu" and "Aloha Oe."

As the last strains of "Aloha Oe" were being sung, Akana, as the bearer of the urn, took his position in the lead canoe. When he gave the signal, the lead canoe pushed out to sea, and the other canoes followed in a line behind. Out past a spot known as the Blow Hole (so named because a large coral head blows up sand when big waves roll in), and beyond First Break, the canoes fanned out and formed a circle. After a short prayer, and sometimes more singing, the ashes were scattered on the water, followed by the flowers. When the beachboys broke circle, the flowers they left behind formed a lei. The beachboys then turned and, shouting, raced toward shore, dedicating the wave they rode in to the departed surfer.

Not all beachboys have been buried at sea. When Dude Miller, the legendary captain of Hui Nalu, passed away in 1935, at age forty-nine, he was buried at the Nuuanu Cemetery above downtown Honolulu. In his honor, however, the newspaper noted that "Hui Nalu members were preparing a huge flower surfboard, all of white ginger and with 'Dude's' name spelled in yellow *ilima.*"

The beauty and heartfelt quality of the beachboy funeral service has prompted others—wives, friends, relatives, even tourists—to be buried at Waikiki. The Reverend Abraham Akaka, who has presided over a number of beachboy funerals, recalled the service that was held for legendary Island entertainer Kui Lee. The composer of the classic "I'll Remember You" and other popular hits, Lee died of cancer in 1966. As a

The Reverend Abraham Akaka presides over the funeral of Panama Dave Baptiste in 1967. Wearing leis (behind Akaka's outstretched arm) are Chick Daniels and Turkey Love. Photo by T. Umeda, courtesy of the *Honolulu Advertiser.* (Opposite page) Years before his death, Panama Dave predicted that his funeral would be the biggest Waikiki had ever seen. And it was. Photo courtesy of the *Honolulu Star-Bulletin.*

youth, he had spent time on the beach, where he loved to surf and play music. According to Akaka, Lee insisted that he not be cremated. "Kui had holes drilled in the bottom of the metal casket that took him out to sea," said Akaka. "I can still remember him saying, 'I want the fishes to have me.'"

Not all beachboys went so willingly. Barbara Robello, the former wife of beachboy Harry Robello, recalled that her father, Bill ("Tarball") Kahanamoku, had a tough time deciding whether to be buried at Waikiki with his brothers or along side his former wife. Tarball met and courted Mary Loretta Davis around the time of the 1931 Massie Case. Davis worked as a switchboard operator at the Moana Hotel, and because of the racial tensions that resulted from the case, Tarball had to walk on the opposite side of the street when he escorted her home. Although the two had been divorced for many years when Davis died in 1981, Tarball told his daughter that he wanted to be buried "next to Momma." His daughter, however, had a better idea. After her father died, she had her mother's grave dug up and arranged for the both of them to be buried at sea.

For many beachboys, no distance has been too great to travel for a proper beachboy funeral. When Scooter Boy Kaopuiki died in 1985 he was living in Franklin, North Carolina. Scooter Boy had left Hawaii after marrying in the late 1950s. During his life, he had been a Pearl Harbor fireman and the Islands' amateur welterweight boxing champion, but at heart he was always a beachboy. Three months before his death, at age seventy-four, he had taken up hang gliding. When he died after falling from a bridge while hiking in the North Carolina mountains, his ashes were flown to Honolulu and taken out beyond the reef.

The decision to be buried at Waikiki was at first a statement of a beachboy's relationship to the ocean. But over the years, as more and more beachboys were taken out there, the ceremony took on an added meaning. A beachboy was not just going back to the ocean. He was going back to be with his friends. They are all out there, of course. Dad and Duke, Chick and Panama, Tarball and Tough Bill, Scooter Boy and Sandy. They have all gone home, to that final resting place beyond the reef.

The funeral for John "Nabox" Napahu, captain of the lifeguards, in 1938. After the last strains of "Aloha Oe," Joe Akana (seated in the canoe bearing the urn) gave the signal and the lead canoe pushed out to sea. Photo courtesy of Joe Akana. (Opposite page) Friends and relatives mourn the passing of Hiram Anahu in 1949. This photo first appeared in the April 1949 edition of *Paradise of the Pacific* magazine, accompanying the article "Aloha at Waikiki." Photo by Jean Scott MacKellar, courtesy of *Honolulu Magazine.*

Not all beachboys were buried at sea. When Dude Miller, legendary captain of Hui Nalu, died in 1935, he was buried at the Nuuanu Cemetery above downtown Honolulu. In his honor, however, the beachboys prepared a huge flower surfboard (at rear) made of white ginger. Photo by Joe Akana; hand-colored by Ron Hudson. (Following spread) Panama Dave's ashes are taken out to sea in 1967. For a beachboy, the ocean is the one constant, the one thing he knows he can go back to. Photo courtesy of the *Honolulu Star-Bulletin*.

REFERENCE NOTES

Duke's canoe paddle, photographed on Molokai at the home of Melvin Paoa. Photo by Grady Timmons.

Introduction: First Break

"Without these remarkable people the island would be nothing....": James Michener, *Return to Paradise*, (New York: Random House, 1951), pp. 48-49.

"schizophrenic terms": Henry Kim, "The Waikiki Beachboy: Changing Attitudes and Behavior," Master's thesis, University of Hawaii, 1966, p. 124.

"curving in a gentle, flesh-covered arc....": Herb Caen, "Waikiki Wicky Wacky," *Honolulu Advertiser*, August 16, 1956, p. B-7.

"Of course, you've met Dad....": Sarah Park, "In the Surf," *Honolulu Star-Bulletin*, September 12, 1953, Hawaiian Life Section, p. 23.

Chapter One: Waves of Change

"Now the beachboy is the final word....": Arthur Godfrey as told to Eddie Sherman, "Godfrey Warns Hawaii," *Honolulu Advertiser*, August 23, 1959, Hawaiian Holiday Section, p. 8.

"The sport of surf riding possessed a grand fascination....": Nathaniel B. Emerson, "Causes of the Decline of Ancient Hawaiian Sports," *The Friend*, August 1892, p. 23.

"small boys of limited means": Alexander Hume Ford, "Out-Door Allurements," *Thrum's Hawaiian Almanac and Annual for 1911*, p. 143.

"Such dues made it possible for every kid with guts....": Leonard Lueras, *Surfing, The Ultimate Pleasure*, (Honolulu: Emphasis International, 1984), p. 73.

"He scorned the surf....": ibid, p. 73.

"When it had been fairly demonstrated....": "Riding the Surfboard," *Mid-Pacific Magazine*, February 1911, p. 158.

"In their leisure moments the beachboys array themselves in outlandish costumes....": Frances Parkinson Keyes, "Hawaii Gets Under Their Skin," *Paradise of the Pacific*, September 1926, p. 29.

The beachboys have had many romances with rich American women....": "'Living Dynamite' Is In Wait At Waikiki, Says Dorothy Mackaill," *Honolulu Star-Bulletin*, January 29, 1932, p. 4.

For more information on William Mullahey see: Kenneth J. Pratt: "Interview: William Justin Mullahey," Outrigger Canoe Club Oral History Project, May 6, 1980.

"dog-gonest surfer": Margie Stone, "Along the Miracle Mile," *Honolulu Star-Bulletin*, May 4, 1957, Hawaiian Life Section, p. 10.

"The Outrigger guys had no problem making a living....": Interview with beachboy Barry Napoleon.

"Waikiki's become a Coney Island with palm trees....": "Act Now to Save Waikiki, Cautions Arthur Godfrey," *Honolulu Star-Bulletin*, August 13, 1959, p. 23.

Chapter Two: Watermen

"Far out to the opalescent horizon....": Frances Parkinson Keyes, "Hawaii Gets Under Their Skin," *Paradise of the Pacific*, September 1926, p. 29.

"long in forming, slow to break....": Duke Paoa Kahanamoku, "Riding the Surfboard," *Mid-Pacific Magazine*, January 1911, p. 3.

"the most versatile and seaworthy roughwater craft ....": Tommy Holmes, *The Hawaiian Canoe*, (Hanalei: Editions Limited, 1981), jacket notes.

"I have seen a man skilled in steering sharks....": Samuel Kamakau, *The Works of the People of Old*, trans. Mary K. Pukui, (Honolulu: Bishop Museum Press, 1976), p. 88.

"the head of the eel would appear between the fingers....": ibid, pp. 86-87.

"Their boldness and dexterity in diving....": John Turnball, *A Voyage Round the World in the Years 1800, 1801, 1802, 1803, and 1804*, (London: T. Gillet, 1805), pp. 72-77.

"Their fondness of the water is indeed singular....": ibid.

"the man who can walk on water": Leonard Lueras, *Surfing, The Ultimate Pleasure*, (Honolulu: Emhpasis International, 1984), p. 104.

"the first surfer in the United States....": ibid, p. 105.

"He is Mercury—a brown Mercury....": Jack London, "A Royal Sport," *Cruise of the Snark*, (New York: The Macmillan Company, 1911), p. 76.

For more information about Tom Blake and the making of the hollow surfboard see: Tom Blake, *Hawaiian Surfboard*, (Honolulu: Paradise of the Pacific Press, 1935).

For more information on surfboard polo see: Francois D.' Eliscu, "Hawaii Originates a New Sport," *Paradise of the Pacific*, May 1929, pp. 4-5.

For more information on Buster Crabbe's Hawaiian youth see: William Oscar Johnson, "A Star Was Born," *Sports Illustrated*, July 18, 1984, pp. 137-159.

For more information on the first modern day regatta for canoes held at Napoopoo on the island of Hawaii see: Tommy Holmes, *The Hawaiian Canoe*, (Hanalei: Editions Limited, 1981), p. 139.

For more information on Gene "Tarzan" Smith's paddling of the Hawaiian island chain on a surfboard see: "Tarzan Smith Paddles from Hawaii to Maui," *Honolulu Advertiser*, November 2, 1945, p. 12.

For more information on John Kelly's witnessing an attempt by a crew of beachboys to ride 20-foot Castle's Surf in a canoe see: John Kelly, *Surf & Sea*, (Cranbury, N.J.: Barnes, 1965,) pp. 11-15.

"seemingly giving away the race": Kenny Haina, "Waikiki Surfers Cop 4th Canoe Title," *Honolulu Advertiser*, October 16, 1961, p. 1.

"they caught a Honolulu bound current....": *ibid.*

"the most amazing bit of maneuvering....": *ibid.*

"Lords of the Surf....": Interview with beachboy Barry Napoleon.

For more information on Duke's legendary ride at Castle's Surf in 1917 see: Tom Blake *Hawaiian Surfboard*, (Honolulu, Paradise of the Pacific Press, 1935), p. 55.

Chapter Three: Duke Kahanamoku

"I have never seen snow....": Duke Paoa Kahanamoku, "Riding the Surfboard," *Mid-Pacific Magazine*, January 1911, p. 3.

"Out of the water I am nothing": Joe Brennan, *Duke of Hawaii*, (New York: Ballantine Books, 1968), p. 87.

"Mother used to tell her children....": Mary Cooke, "Aloha Is for Always," *The Sunday Advertiser*, October 8, 1961, p. D-1.

"It was swim or else....": Fran Reidelberger, "It's 75 Candles for the Duke," *Honolulu Star-Bulletin*, August 23, 1965, p. D-1.

"He could cradle water in his hands....": Interview with Chris Cusack.

"and I mean they were big": Kenneth Pratt, "Interview: Sargent Kahanamoku," Outrigger Canoe Club Oral History Project, October 31, 1984, p. 7.

"like a speedboat with its prow up....": Interview with Louis Kahanamoku.

"seemed to live way down inside himself": Joe Brennan, *Duke of Hawaii*, (New York: Ballantine Books, 1968), p. 23.

"Duke was just the Duke....": Sammy Amalu, "The World of Sammy Amalu," *Honolulu Advertiser*, February 2, 1968, p. C-1.

Mahape a ale wala' au—don't talk, keep it in your heart": Kenneth Pratt, "Interview: Sargent Kahanamoku," Outrigger Canoe Club Oral History Project, October 31, 1984, p. 8.

"Both men of powerful, well-built bodies....": Tom Blake, *Hawaiian Surfboard*, (Honolulu: Paradise of the Pacific Press, 1935), p. 58.

"And what were you using for stop watches—alarm clocks?": Leonard Lueras, *Surfing, The Ultimate Pleasure*, (Honolulu: Emphasis International, 1984), p. 88.

"the ovation that greeted Duke in Philadelphia....": "Duke Kahanamoku Feted By Oldtimers At Dinner," *Honolulu Star-Bulletin*, August 13, 1936, p. 10.

For more information on Duke's winning performance at the 1912 Stockholm Olympics see: Ted Kurras, "The Swimming Duke of Waikiki," *Sports Illustrated*, January 17, pp. W3-4.

"a beachboy from Waikiki": Joe Brennan, *Duke of Hawaii*, (New York: Ballantine Books, 1968), p. 73.

"the last of the Kamehamehas": Edwin N. McClellan, "The Bronze Duke of Waikiki," *Forecast*, August 1950.

"the most superhuman surfboard rescue act....": Gene Hunter and Charles Turner, "Doctors blame heart attack," *Honolulu Advertiser*, January 23, 1968, p. A-1.

"This is the best time to show I am working....": "Duke Cuts Grass at City Hall," *Honolulu Advertiser*, October 21, 1931, p. 6.

"Chick can dance....": Earl Wilson, "It Happened Last Night," *Honolulu Star-Bulletin*, November 18, 1950, p. 28.

"And what have I got to show for it....": Helen Altonn, "'I Think So Too,' Duke says," *Honolulu Star-Bulletin*, August 6, 1961, p. 1. Also see: Tomi Knaefler, "Duke Woefully Underpaid: Godfrey," *Honolulu Star-Bulletin*, August 6, 1961, p. 1.

"I didn't know then how poor he really was.": Bob Krauss, "Wed 25 Years, Nadine Thinks Duke's 'So Cute,'" *Honolulu Advertiser*, August 3, 1965, p. B-1.

"There is a strange sound in the booming surf at Waikiki....": Bill Gee, "Duke legend lives on," *Honolulu Star-Bulletin*, January 23, 1968, p. D-2.

"The canoes went out two abreast....": Kenneth Pratt, "Interview: Sargent Kahanamoku," Outrigger Canoe Club Oral History Project, October 31, 1984, pp. 14-15.

For more information on Duke's death and funeral service see the *Honolulu Advertiser* and the *Honolulu Star-Bulletin* from January 23, 1968 to February 2, 1968.

"the two had gone out for a spin....": "Sargent Kahanamoku Turns Into Motor; Tows Disabled Boat 3-½ Miles," *Honolulu Star-Bulletin*, July 28, 1933, p. 1.

Chapter Four: Beachboy Party

"These Hawaiian beachboys seemed to weave a spell....": Johnny Noble, "Moana Pier, Fond Memory of Kamaainas," *Paradise of the Pacific*, January 1944, p. 29.

For more information on R. Alex Anderson see: Victor Lipman, "Interview: R. Alex Anderson," *Honolulu Magazine*, November 1984, pp. 55-64.

For more information about the 1915 Panama-Pacific International Exhibition in San Francisco see: George Kanahele, ed., *Hawaiian Music and Musicians: An Illustrated History*, (Honolulu: University of Hawaii Press, 1979), pp. 290-292.

"the beachboys and their singing....": Gurre Ploner Noble, *Hula Blues*, (Honolulu: E. D. Noble, 1948), p. 61.

For more information on Harry Owens see: Harry Owens, *Sweet Leilani*, (Pacific Palisades: Hula House, 1970).

"With the quickness of a tropical rain....": Earl Albert Selle, "The Story of Duke Paoa Kahanamoku," mimeographed (Honolulu: E. A. Selle, 1959), p. 15.

"received nine curtain calls at one performance....": Doc Adams, "Hui Nalu Club Boys Mourn Passing of Their Beloved Skipper of Past 15 Years," Honolulu Advertiser, September 12, 1935, p. 1.

"hand-blocked Panama hats....": Interview with beachboy George "Airedale" McPherson.

"Do you know I dreamed that song one night....": Margie Stone, "Along the Miracle Mile," *Honolulu Star-Bulletin*, February 8, 1958, Hawaiian Life Section, p. 5.

For more information on Rosalie Keliinoi see: Barbara Bennett Peterson, *Notable Women of Hawaii*, (Honolulu: University of Hawaii Press, 1984), pp. 214-216.

"who hung out at the beach": interview with Kulamanu L. R. Lyons, wife of beachboy Splash Lyons.

"bye-bye accounting, hello music and fun": interview with Michael Lyons, son of beachboy Freckles Lyons.

"the guy singers and soloists wanted behind them": *ibid.*

"that lonely guy in wrinkled khaki....": Phil Mayer, "Island Friends Mourn Arthur Godfrey's Death," *Honolulu Star-Bulletin*, March 12, 1983, p. A-20.

For more information on Charles K. L. Davis see: Jerry Hopkins, "Interview: Charles K. L. Davis," *Honolulu Magazine*, February 1984, pp. 41-47.

For more information on Francis Ii Brown see: Grady Timmons, "Francis Ii Brown: The Last Alii," *Honolulu Magazine*, November 1984, p. 94.

"third umbrella from the left": "Isle Columnist has His Office on Waikiki Beach," *Honolulu Advertiser*, February 12, 1951, p. 7.

Chapter Five: Ambassadors of Aloha

"My fondest [Hawaiian] memories....": "Cary Grant Dies of an Apparent Stroke," The Sunday *Star-Bulletin and Advertiser*, November 30, 1986, p. A-34.

"friendship, a handshake, and a bottle of scotch": Interview with Squeeze Kamana, Jr.

"love, freely, spontaneously, and generously given": George Kanahele, "The Use and Abuse of Aloha," *Honolulu Magazine*, November 1983, pp. 116-119.

For more information on Doris Duke see: Tom Valentine and Patrick Mann, *Daddy's Duchess: The Unauthorized Biography of Doris Duke*, (Secaucus, N. J.: Lyle Stuart, Inc., 1987).

"You see more people here, darling....": Steve Wilcox, "Dorothy Mackaill—Her Place in the Sun," the *Honolulu Beacon*, January 1966, p. 18.

"When you saw that pikake, that's a gold mine....": Interview with beachboy Kalei Holck.

"if you treat them good, they drain the parents": Interview with beachboy Alfred "Molokai" Horner.

"beach comforter circulating sunshades....": Natalie Rodman and James Brush Hatcher, *Highlights on Honolulu*, (Honolulu: 1930), p. 5.

"bloodless actors": Margie Stone, "Along the Miracle Mile," *Honolulu Star-Bulletin*, August 9, 1958, Hawaiian Life Section, p. 4.

"We were picking out the guys for the day's shooting....": *ibid.*

Chapter Six: Panama Dave

"Waikiki is really beautiful....": Red Skelton, "Skelton is Wondering What's Happened to Straight Men," *Honolulu Advertiser*, July 8, 1956, p. 1.

"his own kind of costume....": James Michener, *Hawaii*, (New York: Random House, 1959), p. 822.

"This beach life is the only life....": Cobey Black, "I tell him, 'this beach life is the only life,'" Honolulu Star-Bulletin, April 25, 1967, p. A-4.

"Look, out there on the horizon!": Interview with beachboy Melvin Paoa.

"Well, that's the whole kettle of fish in a nutshell.": Ed Sheehan, "It's All From da Heart," *Honolulu Advertiser*, January 16, 1966, p. A-8.

"That's V-I-V-E": Interview with beachboy Melvin Paoa.

"the Kraft-cheese girls" and "that pistol family—the Colts": interview with beachboy Joe Akana.

"I know those Hormels, too....": Cobey Black, "I tell him, 'this beach life is the only life,'" *Honolulu Star-Bulletin*, April 25, 1967, p. A-4.

"I've been on the beach nearly all my life....": *ibid.*

"It's my favorite place....": "Skelton's Son to Isles," *Honolulu Advertiser*, August 13, 1957, p. A-14.

"He wanted to be sure he wanted a haole....": Gene Hunter, "Beachboys Still Speak of Panama in Present Tense," *Honolulu Advertiser*, April 26, 1967, p. D-2.

Chapter Seven: Life's Greatest Profession

"Now she climbed back on the surfboard....": James Michener, *Hawaii*, (New York: Random House, 1959), p. 819.

"estimating how long it would take him to get into bed....": *ibid*, p. 818.

"that rippled in the sunlight....": *ibid.*

"the beachboys lie like hell....": Brett Uprichard, "Waikiki's Old-time Beachboys," *Honolulu Magazine*, November 1982, p. 142.

"I came over on the Lurline....": Interview with Andrea Cassidy.

"To the Westerner, sex is a dramatic....": Eugene Burdick, *The Blue of Capricorn*, (New York: Houghton Mifflin Company, 1961; Mutual Publishing Paperback Series, 1986), p. 291.

"lasted for days": "'Living Dynamite' Is In Wait At Waikiki, Says Dorothy Mackaill," *Honolulu Star-Bulletin*, January 29, 1932, p. 4.

"Hell, we used to live at the Royal....": Interview with beachboy Barry Napoleon.

"swim, fool around, no bathing suit, nothing": Interview with beachboy William "Ox" Keaulani.

"You take all the beachboys....": Brett Uprichard, "Waikiki's Old-time Beachboys," *Honolulu Magazine*, November 1982, p. 142.

"By throwing in the element of doubt....": *ibid.*

"the doctor": Interview with beachboy Kalei Holck.

"I was a fool with my wife's money....": Interview with Pete Fielder.

"the watery aisle....": Gordon Morse, "Mud Weds Bettie on Waikiki Sands," *Honolulu Advertiser*, June 4, 1957, p. A-1.

"The greatest incidence of marital breakup....": Henry Kim, "Waikiki Beachboy: Changing Attitudes and Behavior," Master's thesis, University of Hawaii, 1966, p. 134.

"too many of the haole girls going down the tubes quick....": Interview with Andrea Cassidy.

Chapter Eight: Chick Daniels

"Chick always answered his phone....": Michael McPherson, "Beachboy," *Singing with the Owls*, (Honolulu: Petronium Press, 1982), p. 23.

"They knew I was coming": Margie Stone, "Along the Miracle Mile," *Honolulu Star-Bulletin*, February 8, 1958, Hawaiian Life Section, p. 5.

"People just sort of gravitated to Chick....": Interview with Jerry Hallinan.

"'Hello,' he said, coming forward to greet me....": William Drury, "William Drury Column," *Honolulu Star-Bulletin*, January 3, 1960, p. 5.

"the sand fit their fanny": Interview with beachboy Harry Robello.

"It's palm tree time": Interview with Andrea Cassidy.

"I need some shade": Interview with beachboy Charlie Lambert.

"Just checking your timing": Interview with beachboy John "Menehune" Ohelo.

"The way to stay young is to relax all the time....": Interview with beachboy Kalei Holck.

"petting parties": "Daniels Gets $100 Fine on Girl's Charge," *Honolulu Star-Bulletin*, June 2, 1934, p. 1.

"It's all over the day Chick goes": Brett Uprichard, "Waikiki's Old-time Beachboys," *Honolulu Magazine*, November 1982, p. 79.

Chapter Nine: Beyond the Reef

"Out where the blue water begins....": Michael McPherson, "Beachboy," *Singing with the Owls*, (Honolulu: Petronium Press, 1982), p. 25.

"Hui Nalu members were preparing a huge flower surfboard....": Doc Adams, "Hui Nalu Club Boys Mourn Passing of Their Beloved Skipper of Past 15 Years," *Honolulu Advertiser*, September 12, 1935, p. 1.

Additional Reference Sources

Anonymous. "Beach Boys." *Honolulu Star-Bulletin*, June 25, 1955.

_____. "Beachboys, Concessionaires Protest New Beach Rules." *Honolulu Advertiser*, October 3, 1962.

_____. "Beachboys in Business Create Legal Headache." *Honolulu Star-Bulletin*, March 16, 1964.

_____. "Beachboys Petition to Retain 'Free' Life." *Honolulu Star-Bulletin*, September 12, 1959.

_____. "Besides That, They Get Paid For It." *Honolulu Advertiser*, December 4, 1956.

_____. "George Vanderbilt Plunges to Death." *Honolulu Star-Bulletin*, June 25, 1961.

_____. "Godfrey Raps Beach Boys, Gets Strong Isle Support." *Honolulu Advertiser*, August 14, 1959.

_____. "It's a Dreamboat Gift: $17,872 Rolls." *Honolulu Star-Bulletin*, April 18, 1961.

_____. "Joseph Kaopuiki former beachboy." *Honolulu Advertiser*, November 16, 1985.

_____. "Panama Dave's Ashes Scattered at Sea." *Honolulu Advertiser*, April 26, 1967.

_____. "'Surf Bum' Population Swells Here." *Honolulu Advertiser*, June 13, 1962.

_____. "The Historic Moana Pier Passes." *Paradise of the Pacific*, October 1930.

_____. "'Tough Bill,' Colorful Beach Figure, Is Dead." *Honolulu Advertiser*, September 11, 1955.

_____. "Waikiki Beachboy 'Panama' Dies in Sea." *Sunday Star-Bulletin & Advertiser*, April 23, 1967.

_____. "Waikiki Surf Club Canoe Crew Favored." *Sunday Star-Bulletin & Advertiser*, October 20, 1963.

_____. "Waltah Clarke's Motto Is Fun Before Business." *Honolulu Advertiser*, June 2, 1966.

Baughman, Michael. "Add Water." *Honolulu Magazine*, February, 1989.

Bednarz, Judy. "Modern beachboy mixes business with pleasure." *Honolulu Star-Bulletin*, December 13, 1965.

Bolton, H.C. "Some Hawaiian Pastimes." *Journal of American Folklore Society*, January-March, 1891.

Bowman, Jesse. "A Dozen Beachboys For a Thousand Lonesome Women." *Honolulu Magazine*, November, 1975.

Brennan, Joseph. *Duke Kahanamoku, Hawaii's Golden Man*. Honolulu: Hogarth Press, 1974.

Brown, DeSoto. *Aloha Waikiki*. Honolulu: Editions Limited, 1985.

_____. *Hawaii Recalls: Selling Romance to America*. Honolulu: Editions Limited, 1982.

Butts, R. M. "Sailing the Winged Seabird." *Popular Mechanics*, July 1948.

Butwin, David. "Beachboys Prepare to Fight New Ban." *Honolulu Advertiser*, March 25, 1966.

Center for Oral History. *Waikiki, 1900-1985: Oral Histories*. Center for Oral History, University of Hawaii, 1987.

Chang, Thelma. "Waikiki's Golden Boy." *Aloha Magazine*, January-February, 1988.

Chase, Martyn. "Makua Pilots Waikiki to Canoe Title." *Honolulu Star-Bulletin*, October 22, 1962.

Chun, Ella. "Beach Boy Chick Daniels Keeps Tourists Happy." *Honolulu Advertiser*, April 26, 1953.

Clark, John R. K. *The Beaches of Oahu*. Honolulu: University of Hawaii Press, 1977.

Collins, Wayne. "Of Beachboys, Bikinis and Better Days." the *Honolulu Beacon*, July 1965.

Cooke, Mary. "Mini-museum shows the history of 'a holy place'—Waikiki." *Honolulu Advertiser*, April 12, 1973.

Cottrell, William. "The Hawaiian Outrigger Canoe Club." *Mid-Pacific Magazine*, July 1911.

Daws, Gavan. *Shoal of Time: A History of the Hawaiian Islands*. New York: Macmillan, 1968.

Deford, Frank. "Three Little Syllables." *Sports Illustrated*, January 24, 1977.

Emory, Kenneth P. "Sports, Games and Amusements." *Ancient Hawaiian Civilization*. Honolulu: Kamehameha Schools, 1933.

Evans, Kani. "Waikiki Invasion: Beachboys From Florida." *Honolulu Advertiser*, April 8, 1977.

Farr, Helen May. "Women and the Cruising Habit." *Mid-Pacific* Magazine, October 1912.

Finney, Ben and Houston, James D. *Surfing: The Sport of Hawaiian Kings*. Rutland Vt.: Tuttle, 1966.

Ford, Alexander H. "Boys Sports in the South Seas." *Mid-Pacific Magazine*, December 1911.

Gee, Bill. "Fabulous Kahanamoku Family Is Still Tops in Sports Legendary." *Honolulu Star-Bulletin*, April 18, 1953.

Gosline, W. A. and Brock, Vernon. *Handbook of Hawaiian Fishes*. Honolulu: University of Hawaii Press, 1970.

Gilman, Pete. "Survival at Waikiki." *Honolulu Star-Bulletin*, August 21, 1954.

Grooch, William S. *Skyway to Asia*. New York: Longmans, 1936.

Haina, Kenny. "WSC Wins Molokai to Oahu Canoe Race." *Honolulu Advertiser*, October 20, 1958.

Hale, Louis "Sally". "Waikiki's Wild Waves." *Forecast*, July 1951.

H.E.D. "Beach Boys Sling 'Wicked Hoof' To Win Honolulu's First Charleston Contest." *Honolulu Advertiser*, March 10, 1926.

Hemmings, Fred. *Surfing: Hawaii's Gift to the World of Sports*. Tokyo: Zokeisha Publications, 1977.

Hibbard, Don and Franzen, David. *The View From Diamond Head: Royal Residence to Urban Resort*. Honolulu: Editions Limited, 1986.

Horton, Tom. "An 80th Birthday for a Lady Named Moana." *Spirit of Aloha*, March, 1981.

Horton, Tom and Karen. *The Dolphins Guide to Hawaii*. New York: Doubleday & Company, Inc., 1985.

Hogue, Charles Edward. "Imps of Neptune." *Paradise of the Pacific*, February, 1930.

Ii, John Papa. *Fragments of Hawaiian History*. Translated by Mary Kawena Pukui. Edited by Dorothy B. Barrer. Honolulu: Bishop Museum Press, 1959.

Jenkins, Dan. "Summer Surfers." *Sports Illustrated*, July 24, 1967.

Jones, Bob. "Beachnik Invasion on in Wary Waikiki." *Honolulu Advertiser*, May 24, 1963.

Kahanamoku, Duke with Brennan, Joe. *World of Surfing*. New York: Grosset & Dunlap, 1968.

Kim, Marilyn. *Bringing Home the Gold*. *Honolulu Magazine*, November, 1983.

Knaefler, Tomi. "I Really Want to be Hawaii's Ambassador." *Honolulu Star-Bulletin*, June 2, 1966.

Krauss, Bob. "The Ohua Lane beachboys." *Honolulu Advertiser*, March 26, 1984.

Kurrus, Ted. "Inquiring Reporter: What's the Difference Between a Beach Boy and a Beach Bum." *Honolulu Star-Bulletin*, August 13, 1962.

Kuykendall, Ralph S. *The Hawaiian Kingdom, 1874-1893: The Kalakaua Dynasty*. Honolulu: University of Hawaii Press, 1967.

Leveque, James. "Hawaii—The Sand Men." *Honolulu Star-Bulletin*, June 28, 1962.

Machado, Carl. "The Mighty Makua Retires: A Perennial Winner Rests on His Paddle." *Honolulu Star-Bulletin*, October 26, 1961.

_____ . "Waikiki Surf Canoeists Triumphant." *Honolulu Star-Bulletin*, October 20, 1958.

_____ . "Waikiki Wins Molokai-Oahu Canoe Race. *Honolulu Star-Bulletin*, October 16, 1961.

MacKellar, Jean Scott. "Aloha at Waikiki." *Paradise of the Pacific*, April 1949.

Malo, David. *Hawaiian Antiquities*. Translated by N. B. Emerson. Honolulu: Hawaiian Gazette, 1903.

Maneki, Ray. "Police Start 'Beach Bum' Surveillance." *Honolulu Star-Bulletin*, June 3, 1963.

McQueen, Red. "Sam Also Teams With Doris to Win Tandem Race." *Honolulu Advertiser*, January 23, 1939.

Moffit, David. "Fun and Games on Waikiki: The Beach Boys." *The American Way*, July, 1970.

Morgan, Barbara. "Waikiki Beachboys are Businessmen Now." *Honolulu Star-Bulletin*, August 23, 1973.

Moses, Sam. "Thunder from the Sea." *Sports Illustrated*, March 8, 1982.

Muirhead, Desmond. *Surfing in Hawaii*. Flagstaff, Ariz.: Northland Press, 1962.

Otaguru, Janice. "Interview: Nadine Kahanamoku." *Honolulu Magazine*, December, 1988.

Park, Sarah. "Center of the Beach." *Honolulu Star-Bulletin*, January 16, 1954.

Phinzy, Coles. "New Songs of Old Hawaii." *Sports Illustrated*, November 10, 1958.

Ramsey, John. "Bedlam in the Water: The Traffic Mess off Waikiki." *Honolulu Star-Bulletin*, September 8, 1962.

Ronck, Ronn. "Duke gave Hawaii to the World." *Honolulu Advertiser*, February 23, 1982.

_____ . "The Royal." *Honolulu Magazine*, November 1985.

Rosegg, Peter. "Surfboards and Memories." *Honolulu Advertiser*, June 5, 1977.

Ruark, Robert. "Beach Boys." *Honolulu Advertiser*, January 12, 1950.

Schreibman, Jack. "Along the Miracle Mile." *Honolulu Star-Bulletin*, October 3, 1959.

Scott, Winnifred Allen. "Fashions: On the Beach at Waikiki." *Paradise of the Pacific*, March 1930.

_____ . "Why Do We Come Back." *Paradise of the Pacific*, December 1930.

Sherman, Eddie. "Beach Boy." *Honolulu Advertiser*, August 14, 1962.

Stone, Margie. "Along the Miracle Mile." *Honolulu Star-Bulletin*, July 21, 1956.

_____ . "Along the Miracle Mile." *Honolulu Star-Bulletin*, March 30, 1957.

_____ . "Along the Miracle Mile." *Honolulu Star-Bulletin*, July 6, 1957.

_____ . "Along the Miracle Mile." *Honolulu Star-Bulletin*, October 12, 1957.

_____ . "Along the Miracle Mile, *Honolulu Star-Bulletin*, November 30, 1957.

_____ . "Along the Miracle Mile." *Honolulu Star-Bulletin*, December 7, 1957.

_____ . "Along the Miracle Mile." *Honolulu Star-Bulletin*, June 7, 1958.

Tahara, George. "Constant Nymphs at Waikiki." *Paradise of the Pacific*, August 1945.

Tatar, Elizabeth. *Strains of Change: The Impact of Tourism on Hawaiian Music*. Bishop Museum Special Publication 78. Honolulu: Bishop Museum Press, 1987.

Timmons, Grady. "Woody Brown, the Solitary Sailor." *Hawaii Surf & Sea*, Vol. 1, 1980.

Todaro, Anthony. "Waikiki's Famous Beach Boys." *Paradise of the Pacific*, Vol. 64, Holiday Annual, 1953.

Tsuchiyama, Ray K. "The Orphan of Waikiki." *Honolulu Magazine*, May 1985.

Wilson, James D. "The Hawaiian Outrigger Canoe Club." *Paradise Holiday*, December 1936.

Wood, Ben. "Ben Wood's Hawaii." *Sunday Star-Bulletin & Advertiser*, September 19, 1982.

_____ . "Mourners Scatter Panama's Ashes." *Honolulu Star-Bulletin*, April 26, 1967.

Worden, William. *Cargoes: Matson's First Century in the Pacific*. Honolulu: University of Hawaii Press, 1981.

Yost, Harold H. *The Outrigger: A History of the Outrigger Canoe Club, 1908-1971*. Honolulu: Outrigger Canoe Club, 1971.

Young, Nate. *The History of Surfing*. Sydney: Palm Beach Press, 1983.

INDEX

ACKNOWLEDGEMENTS

The publication of *Waikiki Beachboy* marks the completion of an idea that was first broached in 1964 in a conversation among Charlie Lambert, then convention sales manager for Sheraton Hotels in Hawaii, and several other oldtime beachboys. For Lambert especially, who carried the torch from that initial conversation, publication of this book fulfills a long-awaited dream.

Lambert interested Editions Limited publisher Gaylord Wilcox in the idea in 1984, two years after an article on Waikiki's oldtime beachboys appeared on the cover of *Honolulu Magazine*'s 1982 Holiday Annual. Many of the pictures Lambert had collected over the years appeared in that 1982 article, written by *Honolulu*'s Brett Uprichard, as did an accompanying story on Lambert himself, which noted that he was seeking a writer and publisher for the book. In Wilcox, Lambert found a kindred soul. A Hawaiian history and watersports buff who belonged to the Outrigger Canoe Club, Wilcox had previously published *The Hawaiian Canoe* by Tommy Holmes and *Hawaii Recalls* by DeSoto Brown.

My own involvement with the beachboy story began in 1977 when Richard W. Johnston, a retired editor for *Sports Illustrated* and *Life Magazine*, asked me to research an article on the beachboys he was planning for SI. Due to an illness that wound up taking his life, Johnston was never able to complete that article. However, I spent six weeks on the beach collecting information and anecdotes, and when I got a call in 1984 from Wilcox asking me if I would be interested in writing the book, I was prepared.

And so in April of 1985, after the contract for the book was signed, I took the torch from Lambert. Many grueling hours went into researching, interviewing, writing, and collecting the pictures for this book, and I would like to thank the many people who contributed their time, skills, and resources to the project.

In particular, I would like to thank Lambert. A beachboy himself between 1951 and 1956, he proved to be a valuable source of information and stories. (Among other things, he once dated actress Terry Moore and accompanied honeymooners Frank Sinatra and Ava Gardner for an outrigger canoe ride. Later, when Sinatra had to fly off to Kauai for a benefit concert, Lambert escorted Gardner for a night on the town in Waikiki.) Lambert introduced me to a number of people who were valuable sources. He also provided me with a collection of newspaper and magazine articles that were a useful starting point in my research. In addition, several of the photographs from his collection appear in this volume.

I would like to thank the many people involved in the production of this book, especially Warren Iwasa, who edited the manuscript with painstaking thoroughness, and designer Steve Shrader, whose genius for integrating pictures with text (among other considerable talents) is readily apparent. A special mahalo to Elisa W. Johnston, who brought to the

Charlie Lambert

project the same critical and insightful eye I so much valued in her father. Her comments on early drafts of the manuscript proved invaluable. Others who commented on the manuscript that I wish to thank are Joe Akana, Wally Froiseth, Fred Hemmings, and Charlie Lambert. Also Jocelyn Fujii, whose friendship and consul helped sustain me during some of my darker hours. Thanks also to Ron Hudson for his fine hand-colored art work, especially evident on the cover; to photographer Shuzo Uemoto, who shot the studio art that appears in the front matter of the book; and to Marlene Sueyoshi, who proofread the manuscript.

Many individuals provided pictures for the book. Deserving of special thanks are Kimo Wilder McVay, Joe Akana, Wally Froiseth, Harry and Dede Robello, Barbara Kahanamoku Robello, DeSoto Brown, Robert Van Dyke, Ray Evans, Steamboat and Barbara Mokuahi, Squeeze Kamana, Jr., Bobby Daniels, Joe Daniels, Joanne Makalena Takatsugi, Leonard Lueras, Kulamanu L. R. Lyons, Clarence "Mac" Maki, Joe Quigg, Lee Myers, Fred Hemmings, Roy Horner, Jesse Bowman, and Brett Uprichard.

Organizations which contributed photos that I wish to thank are the Bishop Museum, the Hawaii State Archives, *Honolulu Magazine*, the *Honolulu Star-Bulletin*, and the *Honolulu Advertiser*. The *Advertiser* and *Star-Bulletin* gave permission to reprint extended excerpts that appear in the chapters on Panama Dave Baptiste and Chick Daniels, as did the Outrigger Canoe Club, which granted permission to excerpt an interview with Sargent Kahanamoku conducted by Kenneth Pratt that appears in the chapter on Duke Kahanamoku.

Others who provided pictures, consented to be interviewed, or assisted in some other manner whom I would like to thank are: Harry Devine, Jerry Hallinan, Kenneth Brown, Chris Cusack, Waltah Clarke, Turkey Love, Ox Keaulani, Melvin Paoa, Melvin Paoa, Jr., John D. Kaupiko, Blue Makua, Sr., Blue Makua, Jr., Rabbit Kekai, John Ohelo, Buffalo Keaulana, Molokai Horner, Ed Horner, Airedale McPherson, Louis Kahanamoku, William Kahanamoku, Kalei Holck, Barry Napoleon, the Reverand Abraham Akaka, R. Alex Anderson, Charles K.L. Davis, Sol Bright, Michael Lyons, Michael Mullahey, Woody Brown, Scoops Tsuzuki, John Baptiste, Andrea Cassidy, Violet Makua, Mary Lee Makalena, Violet Naone, Ruth Hakuole, Paddy Dunn, Anita Carlisle, Kinau Wilder, Jane Kaopuiki, Mabs Fox, Mary Lou Brogan, Barbara Sheehan, Sherry Riggs, Jim McMahon, Spence Weaver, Lex Brodie, Bill Danford, Tommy Holmes, A.E. "Toots" Minvielle, Pete Fielder, Dave Koga, Randy Fujimori, John Mounts, Mike Buck, Jerry Hopkins, Franco Salmoiraghi, Enay and Lovey McKinney, Reginald and Claire Cameron, Jim and Shirley Rizzuto, the Royal Hawaiian Hotel, Pacific Ocean Stock, the Photo Plant, and The Other Type.

Others who did not directly contribute to the book, but who have influenced my development as a writer and whom I would like to thank are Philip Damon, Tom Coffman, Peggy Bendet, and the late Richard W. Johnston. Lastly, I would like to thank my publisher Gaylord Wilcox, and his partner Dave Rick, whose generosity, enthusiasm, and commitment to the project were all that I could have hoped for. — **Grady Timmons**